For the Recruiting Professional

THINKING ON YOUR SEAT

A Catalyst to Create
Respect, Results, and Revenue

RUSSELL RIENDEAU

3

L

47 VIEW points...

54 - Rebuttals

57

50 ✓ 1/16/99
56 - script
60 - quest.
66 —
67-68 Script
75 income
87 J.O. Form
94-95 script
96-97 list

98 'Top list'

107 INTERV.- QUEST.
DeBrief

114 - counteroffer
Questions

114-115 'money'

115-116 '8 steps'
To AN OFFER

117 Script

118 Shoulder Tapper

119-120

125 'Finishing
Touches'

127 check list
f/ Client Company

Scripts 158 - "GATE keeper"
"
"
"
166

171 RATIO'S
178 LTr to Send
After placement

217 —
↓ ↓ Samples
of All
Letters

READ AGAIN 3/5/00

1

Additional copies of this book may be purchased by
sending $44.95
each ($41.00 in quanities of 6 or more) to:

Russell Riendeau
P.O. Box 1303
Barrington, Illinois 60011-1303

Or to place an order by
phone, please call 847-526-1216

DEDICATION

To Cheryl my wife, for her love, support *and* tolerance for fifteen years of finding-and not throwing out-little "idea notes" all over our home. And to our children Danielle and Grant, whose constant giggling at the title of this book kept me humble and focused.

TABLE OF CONTENTS

ACKNOWLEDGMENTS

There are always a number of people who influence a writer with advice to help put together the best product possible. And there are those people who have played an emotional part in the heart of the writer, and they may not even be aware of the impact they have made. To all of these people I express my gratitude. They include:

My friends and partners, Lyle Stenfors and Tom Beamer, for their willingness to take a chance on a rookie and spend their time to coaxing my talents to the surface.

Bob Mikesell for his constant encouragement and willingness to listen.

Sue Telingator, my copy editor, whose attention to detail gave the finish product much more clarity and presence.

Terry Petra for his willingness to give me a forum to speak and his dedication to our profession.

Jeff Black, my long-time sounding board and creative advisor.

Paul Hawkinson, who gave me space to share my ideas and for his insight to producing a solid product.

My friend, and client, Pete Rickerson, for his constant support and mentoring on how to treat the customer right. And to enjoy it now.

National-Louis University--Elgin Group 23 and Randee Lipson-Lawrence, for their encouragement and candid feedback.

Mike Bramlett, for his vision of education and a role model to follow.

Moe Ross, for her crazy suggestion to get started.

The Nightingale-Conant Corporation, for their courage to work with a new face and to their mission of helping us all improve ourselves and our situation.

My friends and family, especially my brother Wayne, for sharing his passion and insights to the world of writing.

Hal Lancaster, thanks for the chance.

Creative wizard, Doug Beaty, for his cover design on this book and attention to details on our numerous projects.

Mitch Lopac, for his help in getting this book to press.

Thank you John Lumley. You planted the seed for this project a long, long time ago.

Russ Riendeau
Barrington, Illinois
July 1996

INTRODUCTION

When all you have is a phone, everything else looks like an ear.

This comment sums up what the world of recruiting could be to some people: but not you. That's why you have been guided to read this book. Recruiting is much more than talking on the phone into someone's ear.

Thinking On Your Seat (TOYS) is about using your head, eyes, ears, voice, heart, and intuition to become an outstanding recruiter, and a prosperous one too! *It will lead you to the three things all top recruiters seek: respect, results, and revenue!* I have written this book with two objectives in mind. First, if you are new to the world of professional recruiting, or the placement business, as some refer to it, this book will walk you step-by-step through the process of turning activity into income within 24 hours. You will learn why things happen the way they do in the business of recruiting, and how to engage hiring managers to work with with you on a regular basis. And have a lot of fun in the process!

I have tried to inject some humorous stories and analogies into this book to keep you smiling, and help you to realize the fun of working in this unpredictable business.

My second objective is to appeal to those who are currently in the business and have lost some of the spark, or creative drive that made them successful in the first place. This book is for you, as well. It will rekindle your senses and feeling for the excitement within recruiting. The ideas found within these pages are up-to-date techniques and strategies on how to secure the best clients, biggest fees and the most qualified candidates available.

Since starting in the professional recruiting business over eleven years ago, a lot has changed, and not much has changed. Management is still looking for the perfect candidate for a bargain, candidates feel they're worth a million dollars and won't settle for less. But the business of recruiting really has changed. The professional recruiter must be better educated to the ways of business. They need to be able to converse with hiring managers in a way that demonstrates a clear understanding of the pressures they are under. A recruiter needs to have a more broad based understanding of the social stresses and ramifications of unemployment, contracts, relocation costs, and the psychology of behavior as it relates to the business climate. You are not only a recruiter; but a *consultant* as well.

The Recruiters of the 21st century need to act and be seen as consultants and advisors to assist managers in hiring decisions. They must be able to add value to their services to engage and retain clients for longer periods of time. Competing on price alone is history! Low fees and extended guarantees are no longer acceptable means of negotiating for companies recruiting business. If anything, I've seen a reverse in this scenario: companies paying more than the going rate and expecting more from the recruiter. Man, I like that! Whether you're contingency or retained, a rookie or a experienced veteran, or disabled, looking for a new way to earn a living and attain a rewarding lifestyle, this book will help you.

This book will educate you on the behavior patterns of typical managers in big business today, so you can communicate more effectively and be able to identify the right candidate quickly for the job.

You'll learn how to be more productive in an eight hour day than ever before. You'll have everything you'll need in this book to become self-sufficient; from outlines to follow and standard forms to chart your progress; to sample letters to send to clients' and candidates. **You will learn how to earn over a million dollars within the next decade!**

TOYS means thinking on your seat not only in your own office, but in the client's office, or anywhere else. It will guide you to find and manage a certain rhythm or pace that comes when an assignment is going perfectly. There becomes an almost certain feeling within you that the placement will go together when this knowing attitude comes to you. It's the same feeling you get when you're in the "zone" playing your favorite sport, or in a dialogue with a customer, and you know you can't miss. That same knowing is attainable in the search business and I will show you how to get to that stage.

For many years I worked hard following the methods I witnessed, heard about and read about, in trying to find candidates and clients. This process worked only because of the sheer numbers of calls I made to ensure some success. Then I decided one day that I was working too hard for the money I was earning. So I set a goal to reduce the hours I spent in the office per week and increase my income as well. I became obsessed with uncovering and perfecting strategies and techniques that I learned and experimented with over the next couple of years. The results were phenomenal. I increased my billing average, reduced my office hours, and was enjoying myself a 100% more than ever before. The outgrowth of these findings are in this book. I'm not too worried about losing business to other recruiters these days. The strength of our economy will provide more than enough opportunities for all of us. The more I share with you, the more I learn and, who knows, we may have the chance to do a search together some day.

You can accomplish the same results without going through the long learning curve I and other recruiters before us have. The methods and strategies found in this book are proven, ethical, and beneficial to both your candidate and your client. Everybody benefits when you're able to identify the best candidate available quickly.

TOYS is not a easy money guide. It is a serious manual to teach you how to become a professional recruiter. It is not a substitute for the preparation, dedication and stamina that it takes to work in this industry.Like any job that appears to be simple yet rewards highly, there is a price. And that price is study time, practice time and patience. Use this book as a starter book to your personal development library, as a reference tool, trouble-shooting guide, and prayer book; you can't miss.

CHAPTER 1.
LEARNING TO *THINK ON YOUR SEAT* LIKE A SUCCESSFUL RECRUITER

What you are and what you're not

What do you really provide as a recruiter? Do you merely provide candidates for an open position? Or do you provide a bigger solution to the company or the manager?

I see the role of a recruiter covering many facets of the services spectrum. And this spectrum is broadening every year as businesses continue to outsource more and more work. I see the recruiter as not only a placement specialist but also a:

-consultant on issues regarding salary strategy and
         compensation structure.
-skills evaluator for the job in question
-sounding board to management to see if the customer is
         accepting the company representative.
-educator to managers on more effective interviewing
         techniques.
- bearer-of-bad- news regarding public perception of a
         company and its recruiting methods.
 -a savior for the manager, should they be fired tomorrow, at
         least they have a recruiter they can call to help them
         find a job.

> Prepared recruiters of today are at a tremendous advantage over the rest. They can educate, evaluate and effect change within an organization as part of the recruiting process. Managers today are flooded with business issues which inhibit their time to study, explore and learn about market trends in employment, legal issues; and even competitors. Instead, they expend all their energy on their day-to-day managing a sales force, customer service department, or manufacturing. Your willingness to learn about their business and educate yourself on the in's and out's of business practices, makes you a valuable partner to any hiring manager. This book will show you how to market your services and skills more effectively.

As a professional, you're not a career counselor, a private eye for a company, a cheap fix, last hope, or mommy to those looking for a hug and a pat on the back. You're paid on a commission basis typically and that means that the clock is running from the time you get out of bed in the morning until you return home at night. It's your decision where you spend your time, and you'll realize quickly who pays you: the client company.

You provide alternatives to a client that they may have not seen before--that's valuable. If a candidate is in a quandry about whether or not to make a career move after being with the same company for ten years, that's the candidate's problem, not yours. If the candidate needs serious coaching and guidance, then he or she is probably not the caliber your client will hire, right? If you want to earn bigger fees, leave resume rewriting to someone else and concentrate on candidates who are ready and able to change jobs.

Most of us enter this business with the preconceived notion that we will be spending a lot of time coaching, counseling and befriending candidates. We will act as a kind of "Goodwill Ambassador" for our community and family. Yet, we learn very quickly that this is a business of providing a service to the client. They pay us to find them the best. Period. Those who enter our business with "Goodwill Ambassador" belief exit the business pronto when they find out the level of commitment and energy needed to make things happen.

Those of us who remain reap the fruits and have a blast along the way. The moral of the story: this is not a counseling business; it's a business of revenue enhancement for the client and you. If you like the counseling field, this ain't the place. If you like freedom, flexibility, creativity and thinking, stick around.

We talked a little about providing alternatives for the client. Think of yourself as a profit-center. You create profits for not only yourself, but the client. Consider, for example, a sales manager who has a vacant sales territory which does $500,000 annually in sales. If the territory is vacant for 30 days, this manager could stand to lose nearly $42,000 in sales revenues per month. And this does not include the potential lost business down the road since a sales person is not making the necessary prospecting calls to increase business. So you can see why we can provide a way to enhance a company's bottom line through efficient and prompt recruiting. It's also easy to combat the argument some naive managers make who say they'd rather run an ad in the paper for a new sales person. The time and energy it takes to screen the resumes and phone calls, along with the hit-and-miss approach of an ad is very unproductive. Working with a recruiter provides the hiring manager better odds of securing a candidate quicker, thus saving more money than any fee they pay you. TOYS means using your head first; dialing finger second.

Remember; you're better at recruiting than they are. You do it full time. They don't.

Think ME INC.: The #1 fundamental to marketing yourself successfully.

The mind-set of a professional recruiter is one of self-reliance; a personal sense of responsibility for everything that happens.

The business of recruiting is primarily one of cash generation. There's not much money spent on capital equipment, real estate, or Lear Jets, so equity gained on property is pretty nil. As a recruiter you need to be self-motivated and reliant on your own efforts to build your busniess through your clients. Most successful recruiters I've known have looked at the firm they work for as a foundation or a place to build their business which provides a building, an address and phone number. This foundation allows them to conduct business without having to pay the rent, phone bills, insurance and taxes. They work on a commission basis, turn a part of the fee over to the owner/operator and make a great living.

Yet aside from this firm foundation, successful recruiters expect nothing more. They take full responsibility for marketing their services, generating leads, publicity if appropriate, and billing. ME INC. is the only way to really become profitable and independent in the recruiting profession. Be cautious of thinking the company owes you leads, training, encouragement and a safety net when it gets tough. This business is survival of the fittest; those with talent, stamina, integrity, and commitment will make it. The rest bite the dust and reenter corporate America: the land of perceived stability and constant instability. If you like freedom and the ability to call your own shots, then you're in the right place.

What to expect from the corporate world.

Recruiters received a reputation as a "different breed of cat" many years ago. I guess any time your job requires you to work "behind the curtains" so to speak, people might perceive you as secretive and exploitive. The term "headhunter" was an easy word for people to use to describe our motives and actions and it's stuck with us since the early 1950s. It was after World War Two, as the need evolved to re-implant military officers back into mainstream business, that the search business really took off.

Still, people have a mind-set of what a recruiter does, and while we will never fully remove the perceptions people have about recruiters, what we can do is be the best recruiter possible. Eventually, you might change the impressions people may have. If not, perhaps you'll adopt the attitude I use. I personally stopped caring what the rest of the population said because I couldn't do a darn thing about it anyway. So I just go about my business and I've yet to meet with any hostility.

Candidates, as well, have certain beliefs about recruiters--that we only have the interests of ourselves and the client in our mind; that the candidate is just a commodity and we don't care who companies hire, as long as it's our candidate. While it's true from a revenue standpoint that we really don't care who the client hires, I feel that the candidate is important to the process and must be treated with respect and empathy.

If you consider the pressures we face in the business climate today with the crazy turns and leaps in the Dow Jones, re-structuring, and mergers, it's a pretty scary time to be looking for a new job. Then add another element to the equation, a recruiter who is paid on a commision, and you can see why a candidate is a little skeptical about whose interests are in our minds. I think I'd feel the same way.

We need to spend enough time with candidates to allow them into our world of long-term beliefs. We need to let them see that we are just as concerned as they are about the future. Then they'll be more receptive to our coaching and guidance regarding our clients' opportunities.

Getting started

If you're in the recruiting business already you can probably skim this section because you're aware of many of the topics I'll cover. But, you may find some new ideas, too.

In an age where the talk of the day is outsourcing, independent work teams, and stay-at-home workers, the recruiting professional is right at home. Our industry has been practicing this work style for over fifty years and its flexible work schedule and working location options, has allowed people to enter the business world, or stay in it, in great numbers. So when managers try to explain to you that they need a candidate with a self-motivated attitude, you know exactly what they mean. You've been there. You are there!

To become profitable as a recruiter you need some basic
selling skills. You need to understand the basics of feature,
benefit, question, qualify, close. If you don't have a clue what
I'm talking about, head for the nearest bookstore and pick up a
copy of *Spin Selling,* by Neil Rackham, or *SHARKPROOF,*
by Harvey MacKay. Both are excellent basic sales training
books.

I won't discuss the basics of selling in this book because it
would be a whole new book! I'll assume you have some
understanding of what it takes to make a basic sale, and we
will only cover selling strategies as they relate to recruiting
techniques.

In addition to selling strategy, it's a good idea to become
familiar with general business concepts such as profit and
loss, cost factors affecting the buying decisions of companies,
annual reports and what data is **relevant to you working with
clients.** Develop a curiosity for behavioral psychology. Seek to
understand why people do, say, and think the way they do.
Strive to develop empathy for those whose opinions are
different than yours. Listen to their story, and feel their beliefs.
As Stephen Covey says in his excellent book *Seven Habits of
Highly Effective People*, "Seek first to understand, then to be
understood."

Read up on logic and debate. Learn the theories of major
religions and ethnic groups. Study various business markets
and personalities and look for patterns of behavior within these
groups. Why you ask, are these areas of education so
important to recruiting? The answer is simple: so you
understand the way *others* process their world. If you
understand why they feel and act a certain way, you can
communicate with them more effectively, and as a result, earn

their respect and trust more quickly. You'll save yourself, them and your clients' time by becoming a more thorough interviewer and recruiter. Everybody wins when *you* learn.

I noticed most good recruiters have a natural curiosity in these areas of learning. They are less engineering and mathematical types, more interested in the gray areas than black and white. Conversely, I have known some very analytical, methodical recruiters who are excellent and love their work, so what do I know?

Note: As the voice of experience, I suggest you not to read, learn and understand all of these topics in 12 months. It's impossible to study four hours a night and still have the energy to recruit during the day. Pace yourself and stay fresh. Ultimately, you'll learn the most through trial and error.

CHAPTER 2.
SETTING UP YOUR WORKSPACE

The key to becoming an efficient and prosperous recruiter is to work in an environment which is compatible to your work habits and the requirements of the job. In the recruiting profession this workspace requires you to have access to information, communication, concentration, hydration, and networking tools. All this can be achieved by Thinking On Your Seat.

The ideal environment for a recruiter is to have as much of the stuff you need to conduct business within ten feet of your desk. This may sound a bit crazy, but to be successful, you need to make your time count. Time is your money; every hour not working can never be recovered. Whatever wasn't completed needs to be completed another time, thus robbing you of time and ultimately, money somewhere else.

I have visited many recruiters' offices over the years and have been amazed to find a majority of them do not have tools close by that they use numerous times a day.What do I mean by tools of the trade?

This is what my desk and many desks of other top professionals looks like. Except for our own personal requirements, the information in and on the desk is standard to everyone in the industry and vital to getting as much out of your day as possible.

Notice on page 27, first of all, that there is nothing on top of the desk that isn't required. No pictures of the kids, dog, boat, flower garden or big fish you caught. These belong on the back cabinet or coffee table. I try to keep the top of the workspace clear of anything except what I'm working on at that moment. A few notes and files are obviously not going to impede my concentration dramatically, however piles of resumes, notes, annual reports and industry magazines are intimidating, and distracting. And to a visitor, it sends a message of disorganization. I think it was comedian Jerry Seinfeld that talked about family pictures being on the desk to remind you not to do anything drastic or hazardous: "Gee, I'm really upset with that client of mine, I think I'll go over to his office and fill it up with water from a garden hose.... Oh, that's right I have a family, as I see in the pictures here. I had better re-think my intention and settle down. Boy, I'm glad I have those pictures right in front of me!" Kind of silly, don't you agree?

I keep stuff on the floor behind my desk that I intend to read or process that day. If I step on it going home it reminds me to deal with it now and not to let it pile up.

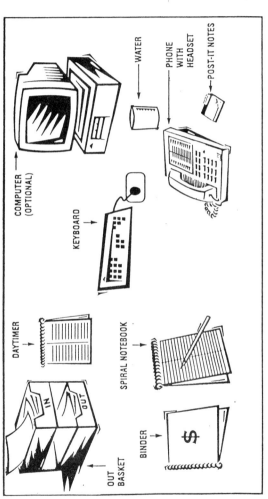

TRASH

COMPUTER (OPTIONAL)

KEYBOARD

WATER

PHONE WITH HEADSET

POST-IT NOTES

DAYTIMER

SPIRAL NOTEBOOK

OUT BASKET

BINDER

BINDER
CONTAINS:
- CURRENT JOB ORDERS
- INTERVIEW SCHEDULE
- JOB ORDER LOG
- SCORE BOARD
- MASTER LIST FOR CANDIDATES
- FIRST INTERVIEW PHONE LIST
- UNITED STATES MAP

DRAWER 1
LISTS:
- CANDIDATE LISTS
- CLIENT CONTACT LIST
- DIRECTORIES
- PRAYER BOOK

DRAWER 2
FILES:
- JOB ORDER FORMS
- INVOICE FORMS
- INTERVIEW FORMS

DRAWER 3
- CURRENT RESUMES
- 4X6 CLIENT CARDS

DRAWER 4
- THANK-YOU NOTES
- ENVELOPES
- BROCHURES/BUSINESS CARDS
- DICTIONARY/THESAURUS
- PORTABLE TAPE RECORDER
- TOOTHBRUSH
- POWER BARS

AERIAL VIEW OF AN EFFICIENT RECRUITERS DESK

Notice the top of the workspace has only one box, an "in" and "out" basket. No trays or stands for files or piles. The out basket motivates us to handle everything one time and pass it on. The in basket (which I have recently moved off my desk so I wouldn't be tempted to lose my concentration when something *new* was put in it) can sit until I'm good and ready to look in and see what's there. The 3-ring binder shown, holds anything I may need in the evening such as:
-current clients' phone numbers
-candidates' numbers
-client list
-affiliate recruiter numbers
-personal statistics of billings, candidate section.
-activity sheet of what's happening that week and the next
-brainstorm sheet showing clients and possible candidate crossovers

This binder goes everywhere I go. Next to my daily organizer, it is my most important article. The notebook is a catch-all for notes, ideas, client suggestions and anything I want to remember but don't have a place in which to store it. In other words, if I need to keep a name, a number, or address, or whatever it may be; I write it in this book. I have trained myself to do this over the years and it's saved me hundreds of hours as well as money and embarassment hunting for information or checking facts.Don't save scraps of paper-period! Create lists on legal pads, use index cards and put a rubberband around them, but pitch the scraps and pink message slips.

Trivial as it may seem, it's important for you to have water near by. Considering the amount of time a recruiter engages in conversation, hydration is critical to keeping the throat moist and clear, and reduces irritation of the throat and lips, if it's excessively dry in your office. I find a couple of glasses of water also keeps me from snacking late in the day.

The Phone

A good quality phone is very important so that your voice appears clear and distinctive. I started using a headset about two years ago when I found my neck and back getting very stiff late in the day and my notetaking harder to read from holding the phone and writing. The headset allows me to stay organized when talking and helps me keep better notes, which is a money-making habit. A headset also allows me to clean-up and organize my space while on hold, instead of sitting and waiting with the phone glued to my ear. Plus, I'm also able to walk around to increase my energy level, stretch and reduce fatigue, and I'm less tired at the end of the day. A good quality system is a must. The cheap ones sound like you're talking from your basement and it'll turn off your listening party in a hurry.

We'll talk about the computer later. The drawers of files, folders and client cards are self-explanatory. I'll cover the various forms and client cards in future chapters.

Good lighting, a sturdy chair for back support, and good air ventilation are also critical to your overall performance as a recruiter. I also keep a microcassette recorder in my office to check how I sound on the phone, from time-to-time, It lets me hear me as others hear me.

I can't stress the importance of having the tools you need nearby to become an effective recruiter. Wandering around the office looking for a thank you card or a new legal pad wastes your time. If you need a break, take ten minutes and go for a walk around the building to stretch. Then get back to the task at hand--your recruiting.

EAR-TO-REAR RATIO-The #1 difference between big vs. average billers.

Ear-To-Rear ratio simply means the more time you spend on the phone talking to customers, or visiting their offices, the more successful you'll be in the recruiting business. Face-to-face, ear-to-ear dialogue is a must and a goal of every professional salesperson and recruiter.

To give you an idea of how to use the tools we just talked about, here's a fifteen minute sample of a day in a recruiter's life. Notice how the tools are used easily and quickly.

Let's say a phone call comes in for you and it's a referral from another candidate. You take the call and as the conversation progresses you take notes. At one point, you reach for a notecard from the drawer and have it ready to get an address. As they talk, you continue taking notes and continue interacting with the caller to gain information as well as possible referrals. You then determine if this particular candidate is worth meeting face-to-face. As the call ends, you write the address of the caller on an envelope, set a date to meet and hang up.

Then you note the appointment on your daily planner, write a short note on the card thanking the caller for the call and express how much you look forward to your meeting them. Finally, you put two business cards in the envelope (one for the caller, one for a friend) and put it in the out basket. As you can see, the process went smoothly and you don't have to remember to do anything else about that call. Now you can move on to the next task with a clear mind!

Successful recruiters go home with stiff backs, sore ears and sore rears--not sore throats.

CHAPTER 3.
WHO YOU GONNA CALL?

" The bear catches the most fish in the shallow part of the river. "

This quote sounds like some old Indian Chief showing his wisdom to a warrior, yet it holds a keen truth; it is easier to begin than you think. And it is also easier to keep going by remembering this same quote.

Calling everybody the first week. Playing the odds.

Starting out in the recruiting industry, it can be intimidating trying to decide who you're actually supposed to call! With so many people in the world, who do you call first? I suggest starting in the shallow part of the river. Start contacting those whom you feel more comfortable with at first. This doesn't mean your mother, kids or neighbor; but a former peer at your last job, a friend in business, a golf partner, friends you've met at parties or anybody who you can experiment and practice on the first day or so.

If your predecessor has already started a file, list, or written on some index cards, you may want to use this information on day two. Recruiting is the ultimate in networking. You earn your living on the ability to entice a person to supply you with a name, information, and trust that is vital to your success. This ability to develop a contact list which you'll use forever is your lifeline to recruiting. And while it's imperative to be kind and considerate to everyone, you'll never be able to help the majority of the persons who call you. You are only likely to place 20-45 people a year, a relatively small number compared to the contacts you make in a single week. You can see now how important it is to focus your energies on the right contacts and not get bogged down on sympathy cases or spending time in markets that don't gererate quality referrals.

Earlier on I mentioned that this was a revenue enhancement business, not a counseling position. You can see already that your role is to find the best possible candidate for the job at hand. **Networking within the wrong industry, spending too much time with a candidate who's not sure of his or her direction or, who is out of your market focus (which we'll discuss shortly) fundamentally sucks you dry of energy and time.** Once you've developed a market to work within, it's easy to identify those individuals which fit your formula for success. If they don't fit the formula, you must develop the personal tact on the phone to let them know they're not right for the job. For example:

"I'm sorry, but my market place requires me to identify candidates with a background quite different than yours. I hope we can be of assistance to you in the future and may I send you my card? (Send two) Great. Thank you for your time and if I become aware of another recruiter which specializes in your experience I will call you and let you know. And conversely, should you become aware of a peer or friend or business acquaintance who fits my market niche

34

please let him know of me, would you? Have a great year. Bye."

This approach is one I've used for the past ten years and I've yet to find someone who becomes offended or put-off by the approach, if they are a reasonable person. It will get you referrals and contacts consistently. And it's the polite thing to do, but it takes time to practice and to build faith in the process.

A Sourcing Menu for finding clients and candidates

Here's a list I compiled of the many contact areas you can use to call people you can help or who can help you. The list is extensive and yet it only scratches the surface, once you dig in and probe for names and referrals.

WHERE TO FIND CLIENTS, CANDIDATES & JOB ORDERS

From a prospective candidate, you can check:
In-house application, if you use one
The resume
Reference list
Competitors
Friends, family
At current place of employment--discreetly though
Whomever referred them to you and that person's friends
Those with whom the candidate has interviewed in the past two months
Referrals. (Note: When asking for referrals give the person a "mental target" of people to consider such as: associations, golf partners, competitors, ex- co-workers. Be specific. Let the person know you're looking for happy, productive people.)

Try to use these questions:
>How did you get to your current company?
> Who do you know that could?
>Can you help me?
>Can I help you?

FROM A CURRENT CLIENT:
Ask about competitors
Candidates they have met, whom they didn't hire
Previous companies they've worked for
Friends in management
Other divisions of current their company
Places where have they recruited from in the past
Other recruiters they have worked with
Their customers
The person whom they are trying to replace

Every question can lead to another candidate, client, or job order.

ADDITIONAL LEAD GENERATORS
Industry publications and associations
Trade shows
Local business magazines, Wall Street Journal, Newspapers, and other appropiate periodicals.
Wedding announcements
Want ads (check out all areas of this section to see what industry is hot and where you could recruit from, or for.)
Company newsletters
Current files in your office
Run an ad yourself and draw all kinds of business leads
Send thank you notes to everybody. *If it moves, send it a thank you note with two business cards.*

> Consider how many people quit, got fired or promoted in the time it took you to read this page. There are always great positions avalible. Call and network to flush them out.

Once you've begun this list, you should have a difficult time coming back to the list because you'll be busy tracking down leads from the calls you made in the first go-around. I use this list when I'm in a rut and a little fuzzy on whom to call that day, or if the business climate is quiet, I use it to re-focus and investigate some new avenues of opportunities.

"Who do you know?" Four words that create fantastic results-- immediately!

This phrase is the most important sentence you will ever use. It must become part of your natural physiology; just as breathing and eating are. "Who do you know" is the single reason you will or will not get the referrals required to make life easier for you. What I have found is that the people whom I think will have a great referral for me usually don't. And the people who are least likely to provide a referral, hand me the perfect candidate! Lessons to be learned: (1) Don't assume anyone is more capable of a referral than anyone else, (2) Have a positive belief that the person will have someone in mind, (3) Always show sincere appreciation for the referral.

Referrals don't just apply to candidates; they apply to potential clients as well. I can recall many times when a referral put me in touch with a friend or peer who was looking for a sales representative or a manager and I was the first and only recruiter to work on the assignment.

Two rules every recruiter should live by

Rule #1: Call those first who can pay you.
Rule#2: Call those who can help you find the people who can pay you.

These two rules are simple and powerful. <u>You are paid by the client company.</u> They are the ones with whom you need to cultivate an understanding in how you can help them enhance their business. When we get it backwards and start to focus our energies on helping the candidate find a job, instead of finding the client a qualified candidate then we have missed the calling of what we do.

The candidate is indeed a critical part of the process but we must remain loyal to our customer--the client. We treat the candidate with compassion and respect, but we must understand the client's needs first. If the candidate does not fit, seek out another and then another. I am always listening for those magic words, "I found this job through a recruiter." These words tell me that company is someone who may need my services and expertise and I owe it to them to know about me.

If it moves, send it a business card.

From day one, send everybody a card. I mean everybody. Send one with your gas and electric bill. Who knows, maybe the person opening the envelope at the gas company has a friend, spouse, or parent in the process of changing jobs, or maybe the gas company needs your services. Faith in networking strikes again!

The Goose Island Brewery, and the $8,000 tip. A lesson in listening

A number of years ago, Tom and Lyle (the two partners of Thomas Lyle & Company) and myself were in Chicago for a Christmas lunch and ate at the famous Goose Island Brewery. We had a young waiter named Matt who was an average waiter, but had a great personality and we got to liking him. We paid our bill, handed him our business cards and said to keep in touch. He informed us he was looking to get into full-time selling and asked us to keep an eye open for him. Well, about a year later, he called us to arrange a meeting and to tell us what he's been doing. To make a long story short, I placed him in a new job with a great client of mine for an $8,000 fee. And as of this writing, he's still with the company and doing great. The power of networking and not being afraid of talking to people pays dividends in the recruiting industry. Come to think of it, Matt even bought us a few beers!

Referrals from the good ol' want ads

Running ads in the paper for candidates is time-consuming, expensive, and frustrating to say the least. Recruiters I've spent time with rarely use the paper to seek out the top people in the industry. The reality remains that top people are known in their industry. They don't need to look in the papers every week for a better opportunity, they network or call their favorite recruiter. It's a gamble whether or not a superstar will read an ad the week you run it. It's not worth it to me. I'd rather invest my energy recruiting through networking techniques we've discussed.

However if you do run an ad, here's how to get the most for your dollar. You can gain a lot of information from the responses you get and the information on their resumes, should that person *not* be a qualified candidate. You can learn who the competitors are to your client company, gain leads to open positions, find a diamond in the rough, and even uncover a few managers looking to make a career move. If you can place them, they'll use you to help them find additional people for their new company.

Specialist or Generalist? That is the question.

Whether entering the recruiting industry or a veteran in the business, the question always arises: Should I become a specialist or a generalist? Rather than try to steer you in one direction, here's something to consider for taking either path. It may help to sit down with your manager or a fellow successful recruiter and get another opinion. There is no right or wrong answer; except what's right for your personality, your city and your business knowledge.

Generalists have the option to pursue any market that's hot. The candidate base is plentiful and leads are typically always around the corner. It takes more time and energy to learn the various markets where you can secure a job opening, so good study habits or being a natural learner will help, if you like the perceived freedom of a generalist.

A specialist is focused typically on one small market segment. They attempt to gain name recognition amongst the managers in the specialist market and attempt to be the "go-to" person. Because the market segment they pursue is a close knit group they must be effective, ethical and visible. They have less of a pool of qualified candidates, but the clients typically want the background the specialist sees everyday, so the placement may go quickly. Becoming known as an "expert" will occur quicker when working a a specialist.

Both have advantages and disadvantages. It comes down to personal preference. I specialize in a few markets, yet I constantly look to find other markets where the candidate I have today could cross-over without much trouble, earn a good living, and create a happy client as well. And in the strong market economy we have seen in the past couple years, clients struggle to find good talent with relevant experience. And are more receptive to other backgrounds. I'm then able to make more efficient use of my candidate contacts. Conversely, when the market is tight as we saw in 1989-1990, companies could pick and choose whom they wanted because more people were out of work and business wasn't too hot.

How wide is your "Knowledge Radius"?

"Knowledge Radius" refers to what your aware of, know about, gravitate to, listen to, want to, or know how to do. It's a way to sort out a direction of interest you'll flourish in. What do you like to do for fun? What areas of business have always excited you or made you curious? Have you ever thought of opening up a business in...?

41

They are questions to help you determine what industries you should consider recruiting for. Sales, management, accounting, insurance, customer service, engineering, manufacturing, healthcare, all need recruiters to find qualified candidates. Is there any one area that seems to fit your personality best? And why do you think so?

Picking a compatible arena to work in is equally as important to your success. If you have a curiosity for healthcare, or a friend who's a nurse, and you loved anatomy in college; then you may have a carved out niche right now. If you love food, or wine, maybe the consumer marketplace is your bag. My Knowledge Radius was that I am a tinkerer. I spent my early working years in the building industry. I loved to build things, plant things, take apart and put back together things, hammer things; I was always a curious kid and wanted to be an FBI agent. So the recruiting industry was a great natural outlet to expend my investigative juices, as well as work with the packaging and building products field, seeking out sales professionals and managers for these two markets. **Careers can be hidden in everyday jobs. Look carefully.**

So what's your passion? Reflect on this idea and see if any one event, place, or environment keeps coming to your mind; that idea may be your chance to a part of that industry.

"Formula fit" and "Comfort zone"; Keys to longevity and success in recruiting

Once you've identified a market you want to work in, whether it be as a generalist or specialist, you'll probably find the majority of companies within that market seek a similar candidate profile. They look for what I call a "formula fit."

42

This simply means that you can write out a list of qualifications a company will require in a particular candidate. It normally refers to:

> average age
> years of experience
> income expectations
> where they live
> college degree
> personal image
> social skills
>   work style

This formula will save you hours and hours of time seeking out the right candidate. If you know that your client will hire a candidate with this same profile the majority of the time, you simply focus your energies to network within this group of candidates and you'll become an effective recruiter in no time. This is not to imply discrimination. Remember you are paid by the client to find them the most qualified person for the job. Your fee saves them training dollars, management time, and lost revenue and potential downtime.

A downside to working within this formula fit group is that you don't extend yourself outside the box. Your exposure to a more seasoned, diverse candidate could be diminished and should your market dry up for some reason, it may take time to re-tool for another market to recruit and place within. This is something to at least to consider.

"Comfort zone" means that you're comfortable working with the people in that marketplace. Some individuals, for example, dislike working with people in the healthcare arena. They believe them to be to clinical and stiff; unwilling to give a non-medical person equal time to discuss things. Others dislike working with the building products industry. The dirt, mud, snow, and construction site visits are not their idea of a fun afternoon and they'd rather call on corporate accounts where air conditioning dictates where lunch will be eaten.

Comfort, not complacency, is important. Comfort refers to a willingness and decision to stay in tune with your situation. Complacency may mean settling for less than what you want, an unwillingness to look for something better, or decision to remain status quo to make life seem easy. If you don't like an industry for what ever reason, seek to find one you like. Period.

CHAPTER 4.
CALLING THE POTENTIAL CLIENT

The phone call goes like this....

Recruiter: Hello Wayne, Russ Riendeau from Thomas Lyle & Co. We spoke three weeks ago regarding sales recruiting for your division at General Electric. I've been in the business 23 years and was the top recruiter in the world for the past ten years.

Hiring manager Wayne: I'm sorry, who are you?

Rec. Russ Riendeau. We spoke three weeks ago. Remember, I went to the same lifeguard school as you did in college?

HMW: No I don't remember.

Rec. Yes you do! We talked about fear of flying? I was the guy who wing-walked the Concord. You asked me how I felt bungi-jumping the Golden Gate Bridge. You're puttin' me on Wayne. Come on, you know who I am.

HMW: Nope.

Rec. Are you kiddin' me? Hello? Russ Riendeau. I'm the guy who dated your girlfriend in college when you went home for break. You threatened to scalp me if I came within ten miles of you.

HMW: You say we've talked before?

Rec: This is crazy. We even talked about your dissatisfaction that the incentive plan is out-dated and your bonus wasn't as good as it was last year.

HMW: Russ! I remember you... The guy in Chicago, headhunter in packaging right?

Recruiter: Yeah.

This is based on a true story. The point of that story is to make you very aware of one factual, unchangeable characteristic of human behavior: we hear what is important to us first. And sometimes the rest enters no-man's land in our brain. Psychologists relate this phenomenon to short-term and long-term memory.

Short-term memory involves retaining information for short periods of time such as: phone numbers in business, locker numbers, appointments; events and information that will not be needed at another time. Basically, it's disposable information. Long-term memory includes birthdays, anniversaries, social security numbers, when to pick your child up at the bus stop and any events that will always be occurring.

> **So the key to moving your calls and ideas from a manager's short-term to long-term memory is to make talking to you stand out in their mind as a very important, positive event!**

HM2L (Hiring manager memory loss): The mysterious virus that causes hiring managers to forget you spoke with them

Think about this for a moment: If you are a manager--a hiring manager and you do not have any employee vacancies within your group, store, company or whatever, you are a happy person I would guess. Things are going smooth and the last thing you need is someone to screw up, quit, die, move, or get promoted. So, what happens when a recruiter calls to introduce themselves to you and describe their services and capabilities? My theory is you don't hear a word of it.

In other words; the hiring manager didn't remember that you called three weeks ago because he didn't want to remember it in the first place!

Having to fill an open position is an unpleasant responsibility that any hiring manager would rather not think about, until he has to. Therefore he tuned out your call and carried on with business as usual. As you can see, the key to your success in understanding and adapting to the world of recruiting is the ability to create intense interest, even when there's no immediate need.

To better understand the psychology of this situation, let's look at how a hiring manager could view having to fill a vacancy in their company.

With a negative viewpoint managers see:
.turnover problems
.paying a fee and justifying it to upper management
.risking their reputation as a good manager
.working overtime to fill the vacancy
.running ads, screening candidates and interviewing
.time away from home
.falling behind in their own work
.customer complaints from lack of support
.could affect their bonus check

Now, what if managers view this same vacancy with a *positive* **viewpoint? They see:**
.a chance to up-grade their staff
.a fresh face that could be a welcome change
.a good recruiter who can save them time and money
.a chance to look like a hero for finding a superstar
.accruing frequent flyer miles interviewing candidates

.increasing their bonus check
.improving their customer image with a conviction to serve
them at any cost
.the recruiter (you) could be their ticket to a better career
opportunity some day

See the difference? Can you find a way to instill these ideals in a manager's mind when you speak with them from the first to the tenth call? I bet you can and it will pay off for you in big dividends.

As you see, the mental imagery of hiring can be stress-filled and unappetizing to a manager who has no openings. This is why they so "no", "I don't remember", avoid taking the call, or are unwilling to meet you until they have an opening.

Through effective phone skills and creative questioning techniques, you can increase the chances of them not only remembering you, but taking your call every time and referring you throughout the organization. And you don't need any fancy tools, brochures, cards, cookies or flowers to do it. *You simply need to discuss what is important to them first.*

The anatomy of a call: seven directions. The most critical concept in search work

When I said earlier that this is the most exciting and intense part of recruiting, I was serious. The process of contacting and exploring the needs of a company and manager can be very rewarding and profitable. It can also be a roller coaster ride for the emotions and the brain cells. A phone call can turn into dozens of different scenarios. For now, let's talk about seven I think are the most common. First, here are some tips to keep in mind when you make that call to a potential client.

1. Expect anything to happen
2. Don't lose your cool.
3. You can always hang up--but don't
4. Don't hang up without getting something or learning something.
5. Keep calling people everyday.

Recruiters succeed when they are flexible with a prospecting call. Don't try to predict anything. Go with the flow, change gears and adapt to the conditions presented by the mood and dialogue. Practice *Thinking On Your Seat* with preparation.

OK, here's seven directions a call can go:

1. It can become a bonafide search assignment.
2. It might be a recruit effort; the person may be looking to make a career change.
3. It could lead to a referral to an even more qualified candidate.
4. It can become a fact-finding mission on the company's past and future, other divisions, and referrals.
5. It might be future business. They have no immediate openings but the manager likes your presentation and calls back.
6. It could be a history lesson of industry, competitors, related markets and their suppliers to check out.
7. You could gain information to market yourself higher up the organization for management searches.

I'm sure there are many more, but these should keep you busy for a while. I have found that when I pick up the phone to make a call and set a goal in my mind to get something from that call, it forces me to concentrate on the various options listed here. I become more spontaneous and more willing to take risks in asking tough questions to really find out if the person on the other end is actually responsible for hiring, serious about making a career change, or is in touch with what's happening at his or her company.

Confirm hiring authority in a manager--quickly.
When you make a call to a presumed hiring manager, here's a short list of questions to uncover any uncertainties in the persons' credibility and authority to hire.
A. Does he or she have direct staff responsibility?
B. Is this the person I actually intended to call?
C. Has this company used recruiters in the past to hire? If no, consider ending the call and moving on.
D. Is the manager open to using a recruiter and would he or she need special approval to pay a fee? (This one is tricky because a desperate manager may want to use you in a big way and hopes the boss will say OK. Qualify, qualify, qualify.)
E. Will the manager hire a candidate who fulfills your typical "formula fit", and whom you can recruit without too much trouble.
F. Is the manager open to discuss the needs, expectation, goals, policy, culture, and pay scale of the open position?
G. Is the manager willing to meet you personally?
H. Does the manager have a current and urgent opening to fill; in other words, a window shopper.

If these questions and criteria are met to your satisfaction, probe for additional openings, set a date to meet, get literature and a fee agreement signed off.

Adding value to your presentation

Remember our short vignette at the beginning of this chapter? The hiring manager didn't recall the conversation; even though he should have remembered every word, or so we thought. The manager did not remember because there was nothing early in the call that a benefited him personally. Your longevity in the business, your MBA, country club membership, specialization in an industry and success in placing people with a company's competitors doesn't mean a darn thing to a manager. **You create value in their mind through the use of effective questions designed to bring out their interests, concerns, opinions, beliefs and values, and most importantly, <u>their</u> career plans.** Once you've created this synergy between you and the manager, even on a minor level, you've made giant leaps forward in ensuring that the person will remember you and will always take your call.

One way to add value to your services is to create a sense of commitment to the company. I suggest to my clients that I travel with them to interview the candidates I have identified, if my affiliate has not met them personally. This willingness to go with them allows me input about the candidates being considered, and allows the manager a chance to gain another opinion before sending the candidate on to the home office for a final interview. It speeds up the process and sets the tone for your manager to use you all the time to help make decisions with them. I also try to spend

51

time with their staff as well to learn the culture and pace of the company, and the job I'm trying to fill. This process gains trust with the client so they are not as reluctant to share information with me, and reduces the fear that I'll steal their best people. If they know and trust me, they'll call me every time with an opening. And keep accurate notes!

You may remember from high-school and college psychology the prominent psychologist Abraham Maslow, who wrote what he called the human "Hierarchy of Needs." These needs included: health, safety, food, clothing, shelter, and self-actualization. The one thing missing from this hierarchy is: for the hiring manager to achieve a year-end bonus!

The next time you have a hiring manager on the phone, ask them, "What will happen to your personal bonus if this territory position is not filled before sales start to slide?" Their reaction could tell you the urgency of the hire and how important the territory is to the manager's pocket book.

Spin Selling

Neil Rackham wrote a great sales training book a few years ago named *Spin Selling*. This is probably one of the best books for those in the recruiting industry. Rackham uses SPIN as an acronym for; situational, problem-solving, implication, and needs-payoff questions. This technique of probing the clients' needs through a pattern of questions is brilliant because the only thing we have of value before we are hired to fill the search is our so-called ability to complete the task. The manager has no product to see and feel, yet our references show the ability to get the job done when working for others,

52

not them, so why should they engage you? Sometimes they need a gentle nudge to take the risk of hiring you too. Effective questions gives them the confidence that you are right for the job.

Using the Spin model, you lead the customer to the realization that they need to do something now, and the simple fact that they're talking to you when they realize this, gives you ammunition and puts you in a position to be the receipient of the assignment. The manager also feels that you indeed understand their needs and how they feel. This techinque is so simple, yet so little practiced in the industry today. We think value lies in form, structure, years of service and education/experience in recruiting. And while these are important facts to convey, they will not, alone, gain you business without effective use of questioning to help the customer see your value. If only the experienced were guaranteed success, no rookie in any business field would succeed. It stands to reason then, that the successful folks out there are making it in the thinking department first; credentials second. I encourage you to get your hands on a copy of this book and embrace it.

Sell The Thunder, They'll Buy The Rain

I think the best way to sum up this theory of perceived value is this: **Sell the thunder, they'll buy the rain.** Thunder makes a lot of noise, but that's about it. Rain is simple, basic, less-threatening and intimidating, yet it provides the essential energy to grow, feed and cleanse our world and its people. Without rain we are doomed; without thunder we are status quo.

Studying for Missionary Work of Recruiting--only work with the saved.

Sometimes you have to do some missionary work to convince non-believers in the value of your work. Here's some strategies to use to get them thinking beyond their old paradigms. Let's explore some of the old-fashioned ways of how managers recruit and how your rebuttal could poke holes in their old arguments.

Example 1.
Manager: We're going to put the word out on the street and see what we can find. Our company has a good reputation and we should be able to attract a few good people for the job.
You: Have you considered the fact Mr. Manager, that with the influx of pagers, voicemail, cellular phones, lap tops, and millions of workers working outside of the formal office, your "word on the street" isn't heard by those people any more? The people on the street are too busy keeping up with technology to be looking for a new employee for you. I recruit for a living.

Example 2.
Manager: We're going to also talk to our customers and see if they know of anyone.
You: Admit to the customer that you're going to send them a rookie to handle their accounts? Let them know at the top of your voice that you have or may have a turnover problem? Admit that you don't have bench strength or a source of talent to pull from in a pinch and you need to have the *customer* help them out? I don't know if I'd do that.

Example 3.

Manager: We have our sales reps keep their eyes open for a good salesperson. We even give them five hundred dollars if the person stays six months!

You: Let's see. If I'm a salesperson, am I going to spend my valuable time looking for a salesperson to compete with me, help my manager save money to make him more, and am I turned on by a finders fee, when I can make ten times that in commission dollars? I don't think I'd spend too much time looking for the person that may get promoted ahead of me.

Example 4.

Manager: We run ads.

You: I like Las Vegas too! Great place if you like chance. If you, Mr. Manager were looking to make a career move today, and you're in the top ten percent in your field, would you look through the want ads for the next career move? No? I didn't think so. Me neither. The elite use networking, reputation, professional recruiters (plug) and personal letters. If you want average candidates maybe run the ads. If you can't afford to waste too much time, use my services along with the paper to compare the quality of persons you find.

These examples can give you a few ideas should you choose to convert the unconvinced, or try to at least. Remember, your job is to find the best person for the best company. There are millions of companies who use recruiters who need you! Find those first. A sense of urgency is vital to making placements. The reality of recruiting is that, no matter what you say to a manager or his boss who doesn't believe in using recruiters, you don't have a chance when competing with the upfront costs of doing it their way--cheap-- and your way, which involves paying a fee.

Sell the perceived negative--and win!

I stopped trying to sell my services against an ad in the paper years ago, because I could never win. But when I started to admit that my fees were going to be larger--much larger--than the ad would cost, it took the pressure off me in trying to sell my services, and even better; it took the manager's main ammunition--the high cost-- out of his hand. It forces him to focus on the value I bring in the way of promptness, candidate accessibility, problem-solving, compensation knowledge of his market, and a person he can turn to if his career plans change and he wants me to help him. Man, am I glad I figured this cost vs. price thing now!

"Oh, by the way?" The top method to guarantee return calls everytime

I've talked a lot about establishing rapport with a potential hiring manager. I've also spent a fair amount of time encouraging you to think on your seat in terms of using all the tools of the trade to create pictures in a manager's mind of what benefits he or she will receive when working with you. Let's review a sample phone script when calling a manager and analyze why it's more effective to establish rapport, trust and an understanding of what the person really needs, rather than our natural tendency to call and promote our services.

"Good morning Mr. Gates. My name is Russ Riendeau and I'm with Thomas Lyle & Co., based in Chicago. The information on my note card says you're the VP of sales for your division. Is that correct? Great! The reason for my call to you today is to introduce myself to you. I'm a sales and management recruiter specializing in your marketplace. I was referred to you by_____ and would like to discuss specifically, what current openings you are trying to fill with top sales professionals."

As you get deeper into the conversation and ask more questions, bring the dialogue to a close like this:
"I've enjoyed our conversation today Robert, and look forward to working with you. Oh, by the way, I conduct searches at all levels of management. Would you be opposed if I contacted you from time to time when I'm engaged in higher level searches to see who you might know that is looking to upgrade their current position or income level or who might just plain want to make a career change? Fantastic! I would respect your input and appreciate your help. I will speak with you soon. Good bye."

See how this call could lead to present and future business? Notice the phrasing of the questions to create an open dialogue, and establish a non-confrontational presence.

The script stays short and to the point. It verifies that you're speaking to the correct person. You introduce yourself and what you do and demonstrate your purpose because you work in the marketplace. You then give a strong referral (if possible) and then lead into a probing question for openings, assuming that every company has them. This forces the manager to respond with dialogue, rather than a "yes" or "no."

If it has gone well to this point, you probably have identified an opening, gathered the job specs and will start working on the assignment. But you're not through yet! Even if you secure a job order, you should still request to contact them to network for other, higher level searches in the future. **This is the critical link in your presentation to ensure the hiring**

manager remembers you. After the call, send the person your card and fee agreement and start the search.

Will this person remember you? Yes. Will he think of you as a professional, tuned in to his needs and the needs of his company? Yes. Can you feel the difference in this call compared to presenting a candidate without knowing the manager or company culture? Does it feel more consultative and less imposing to a manager? Good, then you're seeing the light.

Two minute drill to establish rapport

In any phone conversation you have with a potential hiring manager, keep in mind the steps you take to create an effective and stimulating call. I call it the "Two Minute Drill."

A. Find a manager to call.

B. Introduce yourself as a professional recruiter.

C. Stress the benefits of working with you by questioning if the person values his time, energy, money, reputation, promotions, and future.

D. Probe for current openings and get the job specifications.

E. Ask situational and probing questions to determine the urgency and importance filling the job.

F. Confirm that if you have the assignment and exchange phone numbers.

G. Ask,"Oh by the way?" to link a positive frame of reference to your call and to insure a return call in the future.

If you follow these guidelines you'll have little trouble in getting managers to return your calls and they will give you assignments with regularity. They'll call you with job openings for three key reasons: first, they respected your candid approach and empathetic listening skills; second, they are aware that you work searches at their level and beyond; and third, they are no different than the rest of us; they'll want to make a career move someday! They want to see how good you are.

And you benefit as well. They will call you with job openings; call you when they want to make a move; call you with names of friends and associates, call you with leads of possible openings in other divisions, and they can be a great reference should you have a tough client you need to convince. There is value, value, value all around, when you take this direct approach to managers.

"I'm not worthy."

Many newcomers to the recruiting industry have a difficult time in using this approach we've just discussed. You may feel intimidated by the perceived power the manager has attained in business, or you may feel uncomfortable suggesting they take your call to help you make money. You may not feel worthy to suggest certain methods of filling a job because you really don't know the business yet. Some newer recruiters feel it shows disloyalty to the corporation by suggesting to the manager that they keep in touch with you to change jobs. If some of these ideas are going through your head don't worry. They went through mine, too.

I encourage you to consider the fact that a manager you talk with today will take another job at some point in their life. And the fact that you suggested keeping in touch with them has little effect in the big employment picture. More importantly, in this dialogue we just used, you never actually try to recruit the manager at all! You merely requested to network with them at a future date. If they want to make a career move, who's to stop them? Your loyalty is to the individual (the client) first, a corporate logo second. Ethically, a recruiter never places a candidate with a company and then recruits a candidate from that same company. That's wrong, any way you look at it. But if a manager you're working with at that same organization, in filling an opening, asks you to help *him* find a new job elsewhere, unasked, you can have a clear conscience--you've done nothing wrong. (Although use caution. Should you place this manager and the company gets wind, they may not believe that you didn't steal this person away.)

What if...?

What if , when you call a potential hiring manager, she says right away that she wants to be a candidate for a new job, not a client of yours. What do you do? Start by asking these five questions.
1. Why does she want to leave her current company?
2. What would she want from a new position, other than more money?
3. Is she in a hot seat, on the way to getting fired, laid off or re-assigned to Mexico?
4. Are they frustrated, bored or at a dead-end?
5. How long has she been looking, and what other methods is she using to get a new job?
If you can gain clear, legitimate reasons and the person shows a sincere conviction to leave, get her resume, meet her face-to-face if she is within your marketplace, and probe for recent job interviews and offers. Job offers may show she's serious, and may even turn up some leads for you, should she be out of the running. It also tells you if she's any good at interviewing and will show you the caliber of organizations she desires.

Easy market research for free; How to turn it into gold.

Here's some more ideas and questions to consider and ask
when a manager puts his hat into the ring:
-Who are the top three competitors?
-Would this person want to work for any of them? And why?
(Here's some more leads too!)
- How many other divisions are within his current
organization?
- Can he give examples of friends in the same business,
customers, or similar industries he'd consider working in.

Notice how much questions can play a part in gaining a handle
on a person's desires and position? Notice how much more
insight and information you gain with questions? And even
better yet, how questions protect the newcomer, you, from
getting bombarded with questions about your own experience
in the recruiting industry. How long have you been at this?
What's your background? You avoid temptations of making up
stories when you control the meeting.

Most of us entering this crazy business think there will be
more candidate consulting work. Clients demand a top notch
candidate from you if they're going to pay a big fee for that
individual. So it becomes difficult to give the time and energy
to those who aren't in the top 5% in their field. It is
unfortunate that we can't spend more time with those who
really do need our expertise and coaching, but you would go
broke in the process and our families and livelihood would be
in jeopardy by providing free "round the clock" counseling.

We at Thomas Lyle & Co. offer a pamphlet on effective
interviewing techniques to give to a candidate in need of some
assistance. It's a great tool to show a genuine concern for

candidate who will then turn around and refer another great candidate to us.

Summary

We covered a lot of ideas in this chapter, so let's review the key elements, or what I call the *Riendo's and Riendon'ts*.

-Be flexible on the phone. Expect anything to happen.
-Set a goal to gain something from every call you make.
-Managers are equal to you. Interact with them as you would a peer, with the same self-assurance and conviction as talking to a friend.
-Don't be afraid to ask tough direct questions about their company and their future plans.If you don't someone else will!
-"Oh, by the way' are the four most important words to use at the end of a call.
-Remember why managers don't remember your call in the first place and promote the positives of working with you. Use questions.
-Always be optimistic when you call. Expect good things to happen. They should be glad *you* called *them*, not someone else.
-Don't be a missionary. If they haven't used recruiters before, send a card, say good bye and call someone else. Too many fee-paying companies are out there to spend time converting the rest.
-Seek to understand, then to be understood.
-Thinking On Your Seat means creativity, flexibility, and courage to ask tough questions.
-If it feels wrong, it probably is.
-*Spin Selling*

Chapter 5.
Calling The Potential *Candidate.*

Candidate: The reason I quit was that I felt it was dishonest to look for another job while working for my present employer.
Recruiter: I hear what you're saying , however I can think of over three hundred prominent Americans who not only looked for a new job while working for someone else, but asked you and I to help pay their expenses while they looked!
Candidate: Who are you referring to?
Recruiter: Every candidate seeking office for the presidency and vice presidency of the United States.
Candidate: Well that's different.

Is it? Is it different that they asked us to pay to help them get the job they wanted?

This situation can show how we rationalize things in our life and to realize that even though the candidate's notion was noble and highly ethical; we consider them rather stupid in doing it, because 99% of us sneak around and find a new job before quitting. Right? So what's the big deal?

Who really are the candidates in your market?

Every person you speak with is a potential candidate in one way or another. Even if the individual does not fit your formula, as we discussed in prior chapters, they could be a fit at some time. But how do we sort out the people we can help right now, from the future candidates? How can we be courteous, still say no to working with them and still ask for referrals to someone they know? Tricky? Yes. DO-able? Yes.

Mom told me never to talk with strangers

When you make a call to a person, regardless of how or where you received their name, it's important to set a positive tone with that individual as soon as possible in the conversation. People in sales, management, customer service, engineering and marketing get calls from recruiters on a regular basis, so they become hardened to attempts to extract information or to get them to consider the job you are trying to fill. As a person who thinks on your seat, you will be able to disarm their wall of doubt and create a mutual dialogue that will open doors for both of you.

Remember in the last chapter, the five rules to live by in making a call to a potential client? Well, those same rules apply when calling a potential candidate. They are:
1. Expect anything to happen.
2. Don't lose your cool.
3. You can always hang up.
4. Don't hang up without getting or learning something.
5. Keep calling everyday.

These simple rules will keep you open to consider what the candidate is really looking for from both you, and life in general. Contacting people in your select marketplace and starting a dialogue can lead to...
A. A personal visit .
B. Leads to other job openings they have already interviewed for.
C. Former companies they worked for which could become .job order leads.
D. Information on how they found their last few jobs.(If they were placed by a recruiter, they're probably pretty good.)

E. Friends, relatives, industry contacts

F. Information on industry, competitors, other divisions or other people within the company looking to make a change.

G. A relationship with someone who could be a future manager due for a promotion.

The list of possibilities is endless and this fact-finding aspect of the recruiter's world is the easiest and the most productive part of your job. Through effective questioning practices you can save hundreds of hours in cold calling out of industry publications, newsletters, yellow pages, mailing lists, and want ads. I find that I can spend one day of calling candidates in my marketplace per week and never have to pick up a directory to find a good job order, or potential candidate for a position I'm currently working on. It's *that* effective.

The reason why more new recruiters don't use this technique right away is that they don't have the confidence in their ability to question effectively for gathering names. I know how difficult it is to call a total stranger and say, "Hello, my name is Russ and I'm a professional recruiter. I need your help to find a talented person to help me make tons of money. Can I pick your brain for a minute?" Click. I'd hang up, too, if I received a call like this, and that's what many newcomers do. I've some ideas that will work perfectly for you, saving you time and aggravation and increasing your placement ratio.

What are you really selling as a recruiter? Sounding like an ATM.

I view myself as a "professional shoulder tapper." I'm a person who surfs the employment world within my little marketplace, seeking out opportunities which will allow people to grow with an organization, earn a decent living, improve their lot in life and allow them to do what they like to do. Period. There's not much more I can provide as a recruiter as far as I know. And if I can convey my simple philosophy of recruiting to a potential candidate with enthusiasm and conviction, I've a good chance of them working with me to help find a person with the right background, or entice them enough to consider the opportunity I'm working on for themselves. If I come across as an ATM (Automatic Teller Machine) I sound like a know-it-all and a doubting parent. You need to listen actively to what is important to them and their career.

Sex, money, and personal goals. Do we dare discuss?

Three things that most of us do not share openly on a regular basis; our W2 amount, our sexual desires, and our true goals in life. *And we, as recruiters, ask people about two of the three on a regular basis!* Can you see why some individuals don't like us to call and ask questions? Sensitivity is a must in this probing and invasive business. A sense of trust is needed to be satisfied in *your* role and be effective as well, because if you are to really enjoy and embrace this business, you will want to feel close to the people you work with. This is part of the heart and soul of a professional, and people can feel these vibrations come from you.

What we sell, is the opportunity for a people to see beyond the box they work in; to explore other industries and worlds they never considered. We sell the future even with its uncertainy; we allow individuals a glance at how it could be for them. And all because of our commitment to probe, investigate and explore new companies for growth and old companies for a renaissance of value.

When I have a bad week or a slow month and start to doubt my importance and purpose in this business, I think back to the people for whom I've found new and better employment. I realize that had it not been for me seeing their talent within and finding a company with opportunity, that person wouldn't be in a better home, better company, and looking toward a brighter future. This may sound kind of corny and flowery but I really try to look beyond just the fee I receive, or the extrinsic value of my job. I look deeper to the intrinsic part of the process that makes me feel good about who I am and what I do. It helps to know that I can make a difference in this world, in some way that helps others. Have you ever realized what happens when a sales professional quits a company or screws off for a month and does not sell what is expeced of him? Think about how many workers in a factory don't work if there are no sales and therefore no product to make. Truck drivers don't drive empty trucks and other companies that provide service to that company suffer as well. So you see, we are all part of a great ecosystem living off each other's energy and work.

How to talk to a potential candidate

When calling a candidate, here's one example of how you can approach him or her.

" Hello, Stephen. My name is Russ Riendeau and I am a professional recruiter. I understand you're a marketing manager with your firm. Is that correct? Great! I'm calling you because I am working with a client who is seeking a marketing manager with a (briefly describe position) and I elected to approach you to explore whether you may be curious about the opportunity, or possibly you know of someone who would fit this profile. I assure you everything we talk about is confidential and we can talk another time if it's difficult for you to speak right now. Fair enough?"

As the conversation continues, you can delve deeper into setting a positive tone and assuring the person you're not in this for a quick hit.
" Stephen, I want to assure you that my goal as a recruiter for the past_____years is not to force any situation that is not meet to be. You and I will both suffer and it's a no win either way. So even if I don't fill this opening , I'll survive, you'll go on as well. So please don't feel pressured to take this interview or refer anybody to me. However, I encourage you to think of our knowing each other for the long-term. Maybe another time we can work together on an opportunity. Anybody come to mind that fits this spec we've been discussing?

As the person is trying to think of a person to refer to you, give them some mental targets to hit. By mental targets I mean areas within their life where they can visualize people they know. If I asked you, for example, to help me pick out a good place for dinner, you will start to think of dozens of places to eat. But if I said I wanted to eat Italian, you would hone in on two or three restaurants to pick from. I just gave you a mental target. Same goes for a referral; suggest to the person that they think of persons within their current company, industry, competitors, former companies they worked for, golfing buddies, neighbors, church members. Guide them to see the kind of

68

backgrounds you need. This technique of mental targeting will improve your numbers of referrals tremendously.

Notice I give the person all kinds of ways out of the call. I encourage them , I tempt them, I ask them, and I request of them to give me information I'm after. Very few people will feel threatened or forced to give up something with this approach. They will feel your sincerity and willingness to walk away with nothing; and that willingness is what will draw them to question you more intensely.

In conversations such as this, it can be very helpful to stop the call short.
" Stephen, I have an idea. How about if I call you tomorrow to discuss this opportunity a little more indepth. I have another appointment and I hate to rush through some very important details and exciting information. Is the morning or afternoon better for you?"

In this way I can find out a few critical facts about the candidate and by waiting a day I gain more insight and value. Here are a few reasons why:

1. Anticipation always works in my favor. If I drop a few intriguing details, the person will develop a curiosity to know more.
2. It forces the person to sleep on it and start to consider the reasons for leaving the job. What is it the person doesn't like?
3. Because I'm willing to postpone the conversation, it demonstrates I am not being pushy. Trust is increased.
4. I have time to reflect on the dialogue and answers. Maybe I'll realize this person's not a fit and change my approach tomorrow.

5. The candidate will have the same revelation and won't call me or take my call. This saves me time chasing a candidate who would have probably backed out anyway.
6. Delaying till tomorrow allows me to gather additional information to demonstrate even more of the opportunity merits to the candidate.

Here's a copy of an article I wrote for *The Fordyce Letter*, published by my friend Paul Hawkinson. *The Fordyce letter* is the most read newsletter in the industry and the best I've read. If you'd like to subscribe, call Paul at 314-965-3883.

This article explores the reasons candidates resist at times and how we can better represent ourselves as professionals to them.

"YOU QUESTION THE GREAT AND POWERFUL OZ?"

The 90's candidate is changing how recruiters work....and for the better!
April 12, 1995

The phone conversation with the candidate went something like this:
Recruiter: "Stephen, I'd like to review a tremendous opportunity with you for a longtime client of mine. The company manufacturers plastic packaging products to the healthcare marketplace and I......"
Candidate: "So?"
Recruiter: "Let me continue. I have personally known the hiring Vice President for nine years--great guy. I've played golf with him and he's a real genuine person."
Candidate: "So?"

Recruiter: "What I think is important for you to realize is that the job pays $85-100K the first year and the company car could be a BMW if you want!"

Candidate: " So?"

Recruiter: "Did I mention that the position is based in Hawaii and they'll pay for the relocation and three trips per year to fly your family and friends out to see your smiling face and tan torso?"

Candidate: "So?"

Recruiter: "I have another call. Can you hold on a second?"

As you can hear in the conversation, the candidate had no interest in the opportunity or the recruiter for that matter. Or did he have an interest? Did the recruiter give the candidate a chance to voice his desires, concerns, or situation? No.

The dialogue is a little extreme in reality, but not too far from where we tend to travel in the day-to-day calls we make. We all fall into the habit of selling instead of asking and listening. However the question I ask is: *Is the candidate of today different from the candidate 1,3 or 7 years ago? And if they are, how are they affecting the way we conduct ourselves in our business?*

Having spent the last ten years in the contingency business and completing many retainer searches, I've personally seen a dramatic shift in candidates' attitudes, demeanor, trusting nature and boldness. And even more than anything, I've experienced a greater amount of candidates requesting me to prove my ability, list my credentials, and give them a sampling of client companies.

"Now wait a minute here! Let me straighten you out about something. I'm the king of this castle Mr. Candidate. I call the shots. How dare you question the great and powerful Oz. I can make your career soar like a eagle."

This was my knee jerk reaction to this query from candidates the first couple of times and *then I got to thinking.....maybe this is a good thing. If candidates start to probe for professionalism, longevity, credibility, preparedness, then I will stand out.* That makes sense. So I now welcome the question and think more favorably of the candidate who does question the person telling him what great opportunities lie ahead.

So has the candidate really changed? *Or is it us who have changed?* I think the answer is yes to both questions. In the corporate world within the past two years--let alone the previous ten--I've seen no reason for the candidate to believe our fairytales of long-term employment and "promotions till retirement." Mergers, acquisitions, right-sizing, re-engineering-you pick the word-is an everyday occurrence, and you and I know it will continue. So why should a candidate listen to us lowly headhunters who seem to feel confident that things will be different, the candidate is the exception to the norm? Candidates shouldn't. *We must allow them to realize it for themselves through our approach.*

Consider the fact that more and more families are two income households. And this fact restricts options, when it comes to relocating for a great opportunity, accepting a job far from the daycare center, or a salary that's not conducive to a high mortgage and expenses. Even the top candidates are forced to make career choices that they know will cost them a better job, more bucks, and a major promotion. They realize the consequences of their decisions, however they are making them to retain harmony within their family, for income stability, and for quality of life.

I truly believe that the decisions candidates make today are more thought out than we are willing to admit. We, as recruiters, want the candidate to accept our reasoning as gospel and take the job because it is the right thing to do. *And maybe it is,* but not at this time in the life of the candidate.

Am I letting the candidate off the hook for being a spineless wimp, no guts to play with the big dogs? Yes.... and no. If the candidate lacks the courage to take a risk on a great job then too bad for him--I'll find another one who will. If they are "ready to rock" and go for it, great. I made the right judgment in candidate selection and the fee is on the way to my bank account.

I need to spend less time judging the performance of the candidate and review my process of recruiting. Do I think that candidates of today are more demanding? Do they expect more than they've earned in the way of income, promotions, liberties, luxuries, and special considerations? Yes, I think they are out-of-line in numerous cases. But what I think doesn't matter. It's what the candidate is dealing with right now in their life and what the clients' needs are. My opinion doesn't make a difference. I find that time spent judging is better spent calling for new customers and candidates.

So what can we do to better our presentation with this "new breed" of candidates? Here's some ideas I'm personally working on implementing and improving:

1. Be prepared to present myself as a true professional. Make sure my literature, brochures, business cards, and office are clean, crisp and confidential. Do I present myself as having pride in my profession, or have I let my personal appearance become unkept and disorderly. Has my presentation become predictable, full of cliches, and pat answers? Or do I really know my client's needs and what the opportunity holds? This lack of preparation could reflect that I've lost touch with what it takes to secure the top jobs, or that I won't be truly able to prepare them for the journey ahead. Image is not everything: but it goes a long way in initial impressions.

2. Listen to what the candidate is *really* saying. Are they confused, nervous, scared, ignorant to the industry you're proposing, or are they just plain happy where they're at? If the latter is the case, don't fight it. Move on and get referrals.

3. When presenting an opportunity to a candidate, focus on the benefits to her, not on how well you know the client, how many people you've placed there, or how nice the company is. Give her facts, figures and stories to show how she can fit in. Tell her about the people they serve, the markets the company desires to penetrate, the income potential (real live numbers please), the promotion path or the ability to stay in that job for a chosen time period. Sell the sizzle, not the excess fat.

4. <u>Find out a candidate's motivation to change jobs other than money</u>. If dollars are the sole reason, it doesn't make cents, I mean sense, to change. Nineties candidates are thinking quality of life, not standard of living. Maybe they don't verbalize it this way, but that's the psychological mindset they hold within.

5. Anticipation works in our favor. Give the candidate some breathing room when recruiting him or her. Let the candidate think about the ideas you've planted and call a day or so later. My rule of thumb is: never to work with a candidate the same day I meet them, either in-person or via telephone. I find that letting the candidate reflect on our conversation for 24 hours either strengthens the person's resolve to move, or turns his or her feet to clay overnight. Better I know this now than waste my time down the road.

6. Discuss income on the second date. Too many of us hit the candidate with "What's your base salary?" within three minutes of the first meeting. Give the relationship a chance to build some dialogue and trust. If you've done your homework, you'll probably have a good idea if the person's in the ballpark

on compensation. Patience pays if you want to get real numbers from the candidate. And when you do get to the subject of income, get the numbers exactly. Don't round it off and have everything included in the final dollar figure. Break the income down as follows:

-**Category One:** base, bonus, commission.
-**Category Two:** car, mileage, allowance, expenses.
-**Category Three:** pension, 401K, tuition reimbursement, vacation, stock options (Verify the value very carefully. Candidates sometimes use this perk as a negotiating tool when the stock is worth diddly.).
-**Category Four:** verify what's owed to them if they quit today and would they receive it? Check for a non-compete agreement to deal with or school loan to pay back.

7. Allow the candidate adequate time to research the client company and industry whenever possible. This practice increases your placement chances due to a prepared candidate, and can show very quickly if the candidate is serious about the opportunity. Sending them on an interview too quickly gives them a great alibi for doing poorly on the interview: no time to prepare.

8. Tell the candidate that you're expected to complete references as part of the contract with the client. Uncover any buried bones early on in the process. Don't be afraid to walk away from a great candidate who is hiding something. It will come back to haunt you.

9. Fight the need to control the candidate in the process. We can never really control a person in any situation, but as trainer and recruiter Terry Petra told me, "We can control the process the candidate is involved in." In other words, by setting the ground rules up-front, we allow the candidate to understand why we need feedback, documentation, and accurate references. Tell the candidate it's

to insure their success in attracting an offer. If they can't follow your format, it's probably a sign the the deal won't come together.

10. Be a realist. Don't expect a candidate--or client for that matter--to do something you know you wouldn't do. If the meeting is forced, manipulated, or rushed, it will disintegrate. If you've been in the business for any length of time, you know you'll eat tonight and pay the mortgage, even if this one crashes and burns. Candidates have the same pressures as you and I in their daily lives. Develop an empathetic ear and you'll understand what they need.

11. Develop a genuine interest in what that candidate really wants to do in their day-in-day-out employment. Listen between the lines and probe for what really drives them, makes them laugh and cry, what gets them angry and what makes them euphoric. These insights will show character traits, emotional stability, and a reasonableness which is invaluable in presenting to a client. The candidate will also appreciate your interest in really wanting to know what he's looking for. *This builds trust and may boost your credibility when recommending a position to them.* The paradox of "I'll listen to you, so you'll do as I suggest," is not intentional deception by you, however it can prove beneficial to both parties.

12. Educate the candidate to the needs and pressures of the client, such as accurate resumes, documentable accomplishments, and a game plan of what she wants in her next career move. Let the candidate see that you're not trying to be the tough guy, but the client is simply making you do your job effectively. This approach allows the candidate to feel they are a partner with you in this process, instead of one of several in the stack of resumes to the company.

As candidates we work with become better educated academically, and better versed in what *our* business is all about, we will be forced to keep our skills fresh, ethics intact, information accurate and current.

Our industry has always seen numerous people enter the business for all the wrong reasons and wave good-bye before they really got started. They are the ones who create the distrust and perception of immediate gratification. If we maintain our values and belief in building long term relationships with candidates--as well as clients--we will prosper for years to come without too much difficulty.

Learn what a person does in their job when they're not speaking with you.

Instinctively we all know that the way to understand the other person's needs is through listening with empathy. Yet we continue to feel the need to sell, convince, lure, and persuade another person into our way of thinking and doing. The message I really hope you see and feel in this book is that your success lies within your ability to practice a more responsive approach, rather than reactive and protective. To think on your seat means to know more about what the other person expects than they actually do themselves. *You gain this awareness through preparation and listening actively with the person.* Let others speak and use questions to confirm in their and your own mind what they truly are saying and feeling.

Now considering what I said in the last paragraph, it's equally important to realize that you're not an employment counselor or father figure. You and I are paid by the client to find the best candidate available at this moment in time. And it has been my experience that the person whom you're guiding and counseling today is not that candidate. Maybe someday they'll be the one, but not today. Candidates that need this type of nurturing can rob you of time and energy that deserves to be spent on effecting a search. These individuals are very good at getting all kinds of time and information from you and trapping you on the phone for too long. My suggestion: be nice, be considerate, thank them for calling or taking your call and say you'll be in touch, then hang up quickly.

When I find or meet a candidate that fits the formula I work with, and they present themselves as a mature and eager candidate, there's a few things I do to insure my chances of securing an interview and an offer.

-I first log them into my database or notebook under "qualified candidates."
-I take some quick notes related to their background, cultural expectations, business attitudes and philosophy.
-I spend a lot of time understanding why they want to leave their current job and verify that the reasons are sound, not purely emotional.
-I get a resume ASAP.
-I take notes on compensation plans they received and ask what they expect to earn in the next job and what they'd accept if the job was perfect for them.

The following is a form that I use and modify on a regular basis to improve on what information needed. You may have some special questions related to your specific market, geographic locale, or compensation range or method. The form is an effective organization tool to keep all information related to the candidate in one place, compared to various pages and post-it notes all over the place. (I keep all the notes on offers given and reference checks stapled to this form and any other paper information as well. Make the form a different color too, to make it stand out from the white sea of paper.)

Candidate Information Form

Date
Name
Address
work/home/voicemail/pager numbers

Referred by:

Education: AA AS BA BS MBA PhD   School
                              GPA

Present company: Discuss current duties and responsibilities.

Do they have documentation of successes?

Reasons for leaving?

Current compensation

Previous employer

Are you working with other recruiting companies?

Will you relocate at this time? In the future?

Willingness to travel, and what percentage

General information on family, hobbies, interests

(continued)

Recent interviews and industries or occupations they have an interest in interviewing with.

Strengths and weaknesses

General comments/observations

(You may want to consider some sort of rating system to use within your office to help sort out candidates and possible "profile fits" for client companies.)

Prep work: Setting the stage for the candidate's interview

Once you determine the candidate is solid and an interview is set with your client, I spend some time with the candidate in preparing for what can happen in the interview, and suggest ways to enhance their chances. This is not to be confused with manipulating a candidate to say what the manager wants to hear; that'll backfire big time! I'm helping them present themselves effectively by allowing the interviewer to see what they are all about. Some of the items I review with candidates:

1. Questions they can expect to be asked related to their background and the job requirements.
2. Why are they changing jobs now?
3. What are their career goals?
4. Present their current compensation exactly as it is, not rounded off and fudging.
5. Will they travel and what amount of time is too much?
6. How do they run their business now?
7. Is their resume clean, current, and crisp?
8. What dress code is appropriate to the client company culture.

9. Weaknesses and how to present them accurately, without too much negativity.
10. Demonstrating a sense of humor and humility. Nobody's perfect.

You may want to make a copy of this or make your own list and review it with a candidate to prepare for the interview.

Chapter 6.
The Job Order

Selling shoes in Africa.
Two shoe salesmen get off the plane in a small town in Africa.
They notice all the people around them are shoeless. They
carry their bags and samples to the nearest pay phone to call
the office.
Salesman #1: Boss, we have a problem over here. Nobody has
shoes.The entire community is shoeless. There's no way we
can change a whole nation into a shoe-wearing country. I'm
comin' home on the next flight.

Salesman #2: Boss, the place is a goldmine! No shoe stores in
sight and the people are looking at me with wide eyes. Run the
plant 24 hours a day and tell my wife I'll be late for dinner!

Optimism makes sense.

The phone rings in your office and a hiring manager is on the
phone. You've got your first assignment. **Now what?**

Simple-you start asking questions. Lots of questions. But what
do you ask first?

Here's a 12 point checklist to determine if the assignment is
for real and worth the effort. Use this check list whether you
call the manager or they call you. If you don't end up with at
least 9 out of 12 possible yeses, it's a sure sign of a
counterfeit assignment from a hiring manager who is
unrealistic, not ready, desperate, unsure, or fishing for a deal.

Live and die by the checklist; you'll be a successful recruiter for it.

12 POINT CHECK LIST BEFORE YOU START A SEARCH.
Use this list to determine if the assignment is for real and worth the effort.

1. Hiring authority is *willing* to give you enough time to get the facts of the assignment.
2. Ratio of Compensation/Experience is realistic.
3. A candidate for their specifications *actually exists today*!
4. Manager has a sense of reasonableness.
5. Position not open for more than 3 months. (Qualify for solid reasons if longer, before proceeding.)
6. A sense of urgency. Ask how this opening is making the manager's life miserable. If it is not affecting him or her in a significant way, the urgency may be low. Urgency and importance are not the same thing.
7. Fee is OK'd and a fair amount for the work you'll be doing.
8. Access to the *decisionmaker* if you are speaking with Human Resource.
9. Willingness to meet you, if possible.
10. The opportunity is a solid position and the company has a consistent reputation.
11. You are comfortable working in the market arena they recruit from. Is it in your "knowledge radius"? That is: do you know what the heck they're talking about related to the job?
12. Not more than three other recruiters are involved, plus newspaper ads. (Qualify again.)

9-12; Very workable

5-8; Do a file search and don't hold your breath for a placement.

2-4; It's not a job order, it's April Fool's Day

The job assignment DOES NOT have to:

A. Be a job you would accept.
B. Allow you to work for a manager that you personally like. (Respect, yes. Love or like, no.)
C. Be a Great job. That is the candidate's decision.

The time it takes to get all of this information will be well worth the effort. I suggest that you incorporate many of these questions into the process of taking the job order. Pick out what you feel are the critical questions to be answered before you even start to get into the job requirements, then proceed with optimism if these questions are answered satisfactorily. For example; questions 3, 4, 5, and 6 are important in my mind to determine if I want to continue the conversation. **Do verify that the manager has worked with a recruiter before and knows the costs, fee agreement and payment terms.** There are some folks who are not aware that the client pays the fee.

Once you've determined the search is worth the time to take the specs down, here's a format you may want to use. The questions cover just about everything you need to know to go out and find a candidate that will fit the job. I have found, however, that it's rare that you're able to get all the information in one phone call. It may require you to get the highlights and speak again in a day or so. And this isn't all bad. It gives you time to soak in the information and to snoop around your market for a quick candidate fit, or better understand what the client needs in a background or personality type. It gives the manager some breathing room and a chance to feel comfortable with your work style and let them see your ability to follow through and your thoroughness in taking the assignment.

I've had occasion to take a partial job order and agree to speak with the manager in two days only to find out the manager quit the day after we spoke! Or I've found out some things about the company or manager that changed my mind about working the search and informed the manager I could not take the assignment. Part of thinking on your seat is using all the resources and networking you can to be informed and save yourself time, energy, and money.

Review the forms very carefully and take written notes as you speak with the manager. Put a flag next to items that don't make sense and come back to them once you have more questions answered. Some of those flags will disappear as you dive deeper into the assignment.

THE JOB ORDER FORM
(I print these on green paper to keep my mind on profitable ventures. Green = money.)

.POSITION TITLE
.GEOGRAPHIC LOCATION
.WHY IS THE POSITION OPEN. BACKGROUND OF PERSON. WHO LEFT? WHERE DID THEY GO?
.MINIMUM/MAXIMUM YEARS OF EXPERIENCE A CLIENT WILL CONSIDER
.COLLEGE DEGREE REQUIRED OR PREFERRED
.3 KEY AREAS OF RESPONSIBILITIES OF THE POSITION
.3 GOALS MANAGER PLANS ON SETTING FOR THE NEW HIRE
.WHAT'S AN AVERAGE WORK WEEK LIKE?
.*MUST* HAVES IN THE WAY OF EXPERIENCE-AN IDEAL BACKGROUND
.*WISH* THEY'D LIKE TO HAVE-WHAT WOULD BE A GREAT FIND
.ADVANCEMENT POSSIBILITIES AND WHERE AND WHAT THEY ARE
.COMPENSATION PLAN- i.e. BASE SALARY RANGE, BONUS, COMMISSION
.BENEFITS PLAN- 401k, INSURANCE, CO. CAR, TUITION COVERAGE, STOCK
.PAST SUCCESSFUL HIRES BACKGROUNDS
.MANAGER'S BACKGROUND
.WILL YOU RELOCATE THEM INTO THIS JOB

continued

.WHAT WON'T A PERSON PROBABLY LIKE IN
THIS JOB
.INTERVIEW PROCESS
.DRUG TEST, PSYCHOLOGICAL ASSESSMENT,
FIELD TRIP
.WHO MAKES OFFER AND HOW?
.WHEN WILL THEY INTERVIEW?
.WHAT WILL HAPPEN IF YOU *DON'T* FILL THIS
POSITION IN 30 DAYS
.SEND LETTER, FEE AGREEMENT, BUSINESS
CARD
.ATTEMPT TO EXCHANGE HOME PHONE
NUMBERS--OFFER YOURS FIRST (Offering yours
first eases the pressure for them to give up their number.
Home numbers are very private to some people and getting
it can add a sense of confidence to the relationship.)

If you're able to secure all the answers to these questions,
you'll be the best educated recruiter working this assignment.
Successful recruiters never stop taking a job order, since needs
and expectations change in the history of a search. But armed
with this thorough information, the odds of you knowing the
right candidate will improve dramatically.

Keeping your searches organized

When you start to get three, four, five, and even ten
assignments going, it can be difficult to keep track of what
candidates belong where, what file is where, who called whom,
and so on. Paper can accumulate on your desk like snow on a
mountain. I use manila files with the company name I'm
working with on the tab and I keep all relevant information

inside; brochures, annual report, potential resumes, job order and important phone numbers. I write all over the folder and have learned to trust my system that if it's important, I write it on the folder, not on a note that can disappear. I hate little notes all over the place; it drives me crazy. I like to transfer all the little note scraps onto a legal pad and keep it in the file.

This file system helps me to feel more in control and I can focus my energies better when I have only one file on my desk at a time, with the others on the floor or on the back credenza. It also eliminates the chances of misplacing documents and I can put the file in my briefcase and take it home in a hurry, or take it to meet the hiring manager to show what's going on.

One of the senior partners in our company, Lyle Stenfors, had a great idea which we've implemented this year, and that's to have the job order form printed right on the manila folder to insure its use and eliminate one more piece of paper.

Listen to what the client isn't telling you.
That's what you need to know to
fill the job.

Chapter 7.
Recruiting The Easy Way

The ability to recruit top candidates is the ultimate test in becoming a successful recruiter. Recruiting is the heart and soul of this business as well as the most intriguing and profitable.

Let's assume you've uncovered a search assignment and you've given it the 12 point checklist to make sure it's worth your time and energy. So what? Where and how do you go about finding qualified candidates that will be on the edge of their seat waiting for your call? Oh, they're around someplace. Let's explore where first.

Here's a list I compiled a while ago when I was trying to figure out all the possible places a candidate could be. You will find that the list meandors in reference to sources of people and leads. **The bottom line is: there is no one best way to identify the hot candidates. Start closest to the arena you're working in and branch out as you exhaust your resources and contacts.**

The Sourcing Menu again.

See if you get any more ideas when you read through it a second time.

WHERE TO FIND CLIENTS, CANDIDATES & JOB ORDERS

You can gather information from the candidate through:

In-house application-if you use one

Their resume

Reference lists

Competitors

Friends, family

Their current company-discreetly though

Whomever referred them to you and their friends

Who have they interviewed with in the past two months

Referrals. (Note: When asking for referrals give the person a "mental target" of people to consider such as: associations, golf partners, competitors, ex- co-workers. Be specific- you're looking for happy productive people.)

Questions- How did you get to X company? Who do you know that could? Can you help me? Can I help you?

YOUR CURRENT CLIENT can give you leads when you ask about:

Competitors

Candidates they have met, but didn't fit an opening they had

Previous companies they worked for

Friends in management

Other divisions of current company

Where have they recruited from in the past?

Other recruiters they have worked with

Their customers

If a position is currently open, what happened to the person who vacated it? Call them.

Every question can lead to another candidate, client, or job order.

ADDITIONAL LEAD GENERATORS TO FIND CLIENTS AND CANDIDATES

Industry publications and associations

Trade shows

Local business magazines, Wall Street Journal and other periodicals

Wedding announcements

Want ads- check out all areas of this section to see what industry is hot and where you could recruit from, or for.

Company newsletters

Current files in your office

Run an ad yourself and draw all kinds of talent and business leads

Send thank you notes to everybody. *If it moves, send it a thank you note with two business cards.*

Consider how many people quit, got fired or promoted in the time it took you to read this page. There are always great positions available. Calls and networking flush them out. This is the creative mentality of *Thinking On Your Seat.*

With a reference base of this extent to search out candidates, you should have no trouble in locating a number of qualified people in no time. If an assignment is worth your while, commit yourself to making at least 50-75 calls to source out 4-

---

> 5 qualified candidates. Set a goal for yourself of making this number of calls over a three day period and you'll have a pretty good idea of whether or not a candidate actually exists for the job you're trying to fill.

My view has always been, if I feel the search is a good one, I make the commitment to devote three days to the search full-time. If in that time frame, no candidate surfaces that is even close, I re-evaluate the specifications and either take a different direction in the calls I make, or I contact the client and attempt to adjust the profile we have developed together. In many cases, the client is unaware that the candidate they desire is either too pricey, or is not interested in working for the company for any number of reasons. Armed with this information, the manager can either go to upper management to get an increase in salary, broader specs, approval to look outside the industry, or re-define the job requirements. In any event, the manager is appreciative of the work you've done so far, will remain loyal to your efforts and will value your insight even more in the future.

Creating candidate interest

Now that you're hot on the trail of some viable candidate leads, how do you entice and create a curious environment for that person to want to interview? Let's review some conversation ideas you can use to extract information from the candidate and build trust and a willingness to consider your opportunity.

" Hello, Bob. My name is Russ Riendeau and I am a professional sales and management recruiter with Thomas Lyle & Co. I have specialized in the _____ market for the

past ten years and was referred by_____,
confidentially, of course.(or, I identified you through sources
from within the industry, or, I spent some time investigating
persons within your company and I believe you are the person
I need to talk with.)

Note: I always use my real name when contacting a candidate.
The only time I will use a fictitious name is when a company
whom I have been recruiting a lot of people from, may know
my name and I don't want to put the person I'm contacting in
jeopardy of losing their job by talking to me.

The call continues...

I have been asked by a company to identify a person who can
and will_____(fill in a short description of the
opportunity.) Is this a good time to talk, or shall we reconnect
at another time?"

If the person elects to continue the conversation, it can go like
this....

"I am pleased we can talk now about this exciting opportunity.
Tell me a little about your background and current
responsibilities."

As the conversation continues, press further into backgrounds
and why they have made the career moves they've made.
Attempt to sort out their reasons for changing and where they
are looking to be in the next couple of years. Now I use the
following rough check list to make sure I don't miss any
critical information that could blow up the deal at a later
date.Listen, listen, listen.

1. Review the candidate's background carefully. Get a resume or have the person create a quick fact sheet of past jobs, duties and education.

2. If the candidate says he's not seriously looking, yet he has a current resume, then he's looking and/or isn't convinced your opportunity is solid.

3. What is his motivation to change jobs, **other than money**? This is critical information when it comes to offer time and the candidate blinks when the bucks are not as high as he wanted.

4. Is the candidate serious about making a change, or has he hit a rough spot in his career at the company. Maybe some personal problems are prompting an emotional "quick fix"; i.e. family, marital, children, health problems, elderly parents.

5. Is the candidate willing to interview between 9 a.m.-5 p.m.? This shows a commitment to make a change. Although some people can't leave an office without causing some suspicion, be aware that the rules can change.

6. What does the person really want to do and have? What is the most important element to day-to-day happiness in that person's life? What would the person's spouse or significant other say if you asked the same question?

7. Test the counter-offer scenario. "When you go into resign, Mr./Ms. candidate, what will your present employer say and do to keep you?"
.Will they let you go that day?
.Ask you to stay on 2 weeks?

.Will they try to persuade you to stay, by promising you a raise, better working conditions, and a promotion?

.Why didn't they do these things for you before you had to blackmail them into giving you what you deserve?

Listen carefully to the response. If they have been with their current employer for more than five years, be on guard for a tree-hugger. A tree-hugger wants to leave and tells you she does, but holds on to the tree even though your opportunity is better. The person is just plain scared and reluctant to change. Say goodbye and call someone else.

8. Meet the person if possible to create trust and get a better feel for who the candidate is and how he or she interviews. Remember: people never look like they sound.

9. Agree to talk to the candidate within 24 hours after the initial call. The candidate will become more or less interested, and you will do the same. Time allows the intuition and logic to set in after the enthusiasm of the moment has died down. Impulse spending is a good example of how this approach is works.

10. Don't mention your client's name in the first conversation. Anticipation works in your favor to see if the recruit is really interested in making a change. Plus, you don't want the client name to get out too soon if the candidate is not a fit and tells other people about the opening. Don't create competition for yourself.

Continue to recruit in this mode until you have found 5-8 candidates who are qualified and interested in taking it to the next step: an interview with the client.

Definition of a "qualified" candidate.

Here's a quick checklist of seven characteristics a candidate should have to increase your chances of getting your fee.
1. Top 10% in their industry or company.
2. An air of competence and confidence.
3. Motivated to change for reasons other than money.
4. Have not been with their current company for more than six years.
5. Project a professional appearance.
6. Appear reasonable.
7. Personality is a fit or close.

Final thoughts on recruiting candidates

Remember who pays your fee; your loyalty is first to your clients. They are who pay and stay with you if you perform. Don't force any person to interview with a client. It will give you a poor reputation, limit your future referrals and the candidate may even tell the client you coerced them to interviewing when they really didn't want to. Bye Bye client! Bottom line: if you have to sell a candidate on an opportunity, forget it. If they don't see the benefits, then they view things differently than you and that's OK. Go find another person.

Be adaptable. *Thinking On Your Seat* is about creativity and reasonableness. Candidates think and feel the same as you do when it comes to security, food, clothing, shelter, money etc. They are smart and logical, despite what you think when they don't see it your way. Again, be empathetic with people and try to understand before being understood.

Last note. Keep a log book of every candidate you talk with and how they got to you, either through referral, letter, or ad. This will help you identify, over time, where you're most effective in sourcing candidates and then concentrate your energies in that area. The 80/20 rule comes into play again here.

If a potential recruit shows
little excitement for the chance to
make a change for the better, walk away.
No run away.
Life is to short to mess with tree-huggers.

Chapter 8.
Making Presentations To Your Client

Picture this scene: A group of Indians conducting a rain dance ceromony, while another group of Indians are out back behind the reservation frantically washing their Jeep Cherokees to ensure it will rain.

As in the story of the Indian washing cars in the back to guarantee it'll rain the next day, you need to be confident of your effort in securing a solid candidate for the client. Without a sincere belief that your candidate is the best you have found to date, the client will not share the enthusiasm of the profile and will pass. Hiring managers are no different than you and me. They know when you're excited about finding a great candidate. They sense your excitement about a candidate's energy level, and will agree to see that candidate, even if the background is slightly off the spec.

Your mission as a recruiter is to secure an interview(s) for candidates which <u>come as close to the spec as possible</u>, given the conditions of the business climate and the industry you're conducting the search in. If you've followed the steps in the search process to this point, there shouldn't be a big problem in securing an interview for the candidates you've identified. The job profile should be in place and agreeable to both you and the hiring manager. Whether the specs are open to a background of experience which allows flexibility, or closed and cut in stone, the candidates you're presenting should fit and the manager should agree to see them face-to-face. Let's walk through the steps to getting the interviews going.

Sharp-Dressed Man

You should fax or mail a resume directly to the hiring manager. Preferably send a nice, clean copy without any of your scribblings and doodles. Put "Personal and Confidential" on the cover sheet to insure as much privacy and confidentiality to the candidate as possible. I rarely put any compensation information on the fax sheet because many times the hiring manager doesn't want existing employees to be aware of what a particular job is paying.

Include in the cover sheet a few of your notes and comments regarding the candidate. These should be positive and factual notes reflecting the fact that you did indeed spend some time with this person discussing the future and your client's opportunity. Be careful not to get too flowery and syrupy about the candidate, as the client will feel you're trying to sell the candidate too hard. If the background is close and you think highly of the candidate, the client will probably agree. **Don't oversell.**

Holding your Ace in the hole?

One theory or belief in the recruiting profession is to save your best candidate until last. The belief is that you present the lesser candidates to the employer first and slowly build the talent to a crescendo ending with the superstar. And while this technique can make a lot of selling sense, it can also prove unpredictable and blow up in your face. Why? Well, first of all, it's only your opinion who the superstar of the bunch is. How can you really be sure the client will feel the same way? You can't. What if the superstar you pick doesn't want the job as much as the #2 candidate in your mind? Remember Avis: "we try harder?" What if the client tires of the candidates you've been sending him for the past five hours and calls off the search because he feels you haven't spent time listening to their wishes. You may not have a chance to show them the superstar. Ouch!

My suggestion to you is to present a group of qualified candidates to the client in a short period of time; let's say three days. Inform the client that the group you're sending them is the best candidates you've seen at this time and place in the market. Fight the urge to rank them from least to most qualified, even though many times the client will ask you to do this for them. My response to this request is ,"Mr./Mrs. Client, I would hate to rank the candidates. I know what's important to me, but only you know what's really important to you! The candidates fit the profile you gave me and they all appear interested and eager to find out more about your opportunity. I encourage you to see all of them and then evaluate them. That would be a fair way for you to feel good about your decision."

This approach takes the burden off you to be responsible for the candidate. It forces the manager *to really* interview each candidate thoroughly to see which one is the best fit. It can even lead to *additional* hires because a candidate which is not right for the particular job your manager is filling could be perfect for another division. If that manager had not interviewed that individual thoroughly, they may not have uncovered talents which fit another job. Another easy placement for you! I've had dozens of experiences where a manager hires the candidate whom I personally felt didn't have a chance. I learned to stop being the band director and just listen to the music, or in this case, the manager.

I support the theory of not presenting someone with a perfect background and personality--if you're able to predict such a thing--to a hiring manager early in the search. If you are working on an assignment and the day after the search begins you find a superstar, hold that thought for a day or two. Don't be too anxious to call the manager and present the candidate. Why? Because the candidate may not be as interested as you first thought. The candidate may feel rushed and forced into making a hasty decision that ultimately is on good. The hiring manager may not be mentally ready to interview your candidate. Or the manager may be suspicious of how quickly you were able to find a superstar and pay you less since you appeared to do hardly any work. **Presenting strong references on the candidate can help the client to see the value without you trying to sell him on the candidate.**

Spend a few days uncovering as many candidates you can to demonstrate to the client that you actually work for a living. This time frame allows you to be selective in whom you present and also gives you the confidence that even if your superstar falls flat, you have other candidates to fill the position. Having additional qualified candidates to present also gives you leverage against a superstar who thinks he or she has an edge on the competition. If a person thinks they are the only one for the job, the price tag can go way up. **By tempering the superstar with information that the client is interviewing three other qualified candidates, along with them, the candidate will be forced to really sell him or herself and look seriously at the opportunity. It makes it easier to evaluate who really wants the job and who is just tire-kicking to get a better handle on their value.**

When I feel really strongly about an individual, I attempt to put the candidate who is stronger--in my mind-- towards the

When I feel really strongly about an individual, I attempt to put the candidate who is stronger--in my mind-- towards the end of the interview process. I feel it allows the manager a chance to get a feel for what they need and allows extra time to meet with the stronger candidate.

Preparing the *client* for interviews

Most managers are like us; they dislike interviewing and the whole evaluation process. It's artificial and calculated, and difficult to really know if a person is sincere, full of bull, or a genuine hard-working American. So after you've presented the resumes to the client, spend some time reviewing the background of the candidate. Listen to what clients deduce from the resume.
-What do they key in on in the resume?
-What is important to them?
-Any pet peeves, like social activities, Big Ten school preference, golfer, etc.
-Any surprise requirements like technical degrees, marketing experience, geographic limitations?
-Is the manager easier than you thought in their requirements?

These observations go a long way towards increasing the chances of making a placement. Listening to what managers feel is important will allow you to identify additional candidates easily, if needed, and prepare the candidate to focus on the areas of importance to the hiring manager. You're not manipulating the interview, but improving the communication of what's important to both parties. The interview between them will eventually bring out what's important to both parties.

example, if the candidate is a slow starter in an interview, based on your meeting with them, mention to the manager that you like the candidate, and that they'll probably notice that person warms up a little slower than most, but when the candidate gets involved in the interview, he or she is a bundle of energy. Or if a candidate has a lot of different jobs in different industries, suggest that the client look at the candidate's accomplishments, reflecting a strong ability to learn quickly.

By setting the tempo and mood of the interviews you allow the interview to go smoothly and predictably. It facilitates a quicker selection process.

After reviewing all the profiles; set a day and times to interview the candidates. Contact the candidates, lock them in to a time and confirm those times with the manager. Continue to encourage the client to keep an open mind towards personalities and backgrounds that don't fit their formula. Encourage managers to realize that they themselves once lacked the experience in this market and they have done very well. Keeping an open mind allows greater chances of the client hiring one of your candidates and may allow the manager to explore a new, successful approach to growing their business.

Recently, I wrote a pamphlet entitled *Renaissance in Recruiting; 58 Strategies to Find & Keep Elite Sales Professionals.* This pamphlet was filled with provocative ideas to get managers off the traditional, safe path of hiring clones and repeats of years-ago profiles. It was designed to stimulate creativity in hiring and allow managers freedom to express what they felt is needed in hiring. The positive response I received from this brochure convinced me that clients appreciate new approaches to the hiring process and recruiters who are striving to help clients do their jobs better. Something to consider next time you talk to a client!

Post-game (interview) follow up

Debriefing time."Well, how'd it go?" is the first question you'd like to ask the client.
Some clients will want to discuss every candidate in-depth and share every note they took. Others will say, "I like Sue and Bob, forget the others."

When you are debriefing from interviews, try to set a positive mood to the call. Don't feel the need to defend your candidates --it's too late for that. Just listen to the manager's comments and feelings and take a lot of notes. You'll need those shortly. Pay attention to what they are saying and what they're not saying. Did they like the group as a whole? Was there one that stood out among the rest? Are they unsure who was good and who was a good fit? Do they rank them? Or do they ask you for your rankings to confirm their impressions?

As you go through this exercise, ask the client why they like the number 1 candidate. .What is it that makes this candidate stand out?
. Can they see the candidate working for them?
. Would the candidate's personality fit into the organization?
. Would their boss like and approve of the choice?
. After an additional interview, would they consider making the candidate an offer?
. Is there a start date that would work better should the client want to hire that person?
. Shall you complete some confidential references?
. Whom do the candidates need to meet next?

107

. What does the client want you to tell the candidate?

These questions are certainly closing questions, yet they are not too pushy. They allow the manager time and space to evaluate and reflect on the process and candidate. In phrasing the questions in this manner, the client can't feel that you are pressuring them. You're just doing you job of understanding what's important. You are also protecting the candidate from taking another job by asking what to say to the candidate after the interview. If the manager says "Tell them to sit tight and I'll be back," then the candidate may get an offer. If the manager says "I can't commit right now," then you should consider sending more candidates and let the person continue interviewing elsewhere.

I find if I can ask the tough questions, the ones for which I may not like the answer, then I have a better chance of making the placement. Managers like to be given tough questions; they force effective thinking and bring the real issues to the forefront. If they can't answer the tough questions, then they are not ready to hire, or they need to revise what they want. In any light, you have saved yourself,and them, time and energy pursuing a search that will die a quick death. Better to know today it's falling apart, so you can channel your energies towards a new search, than to prolong the event until you fall behind hoping it will be resurrected.

Set up the second interviews and follow the same sequence of events as the first; question, and qualify constantly towards securing an offer. By now you've spent enough time with the candidate to know their compensation plan and benefits plan and what they are expecting. You've also prepared the client as to what the candidate expects and what the client should consider offering.

Closing the search and sending the invoice

We spend more time on the offer and acceptance in a later chapter. But first it's important to understand the preparation of the candidate for the interview so you can understand the process of putting the package together and making it stick.

Closing the deal should be a very natural, logical process to recruiting. If you have laid the groundwork of a strong understanding with the client and candidate, the offer should be the right number and the benefits all acceptable. If there's difficulty at the end of the search, then you've missed some step along the way, or the manager has changed the game rules. In any event, if you missed the signs, watch and listen very carefully. It's your time and money. Thinking on your seat means listening with a critical ear and mind.

On becoming an expert: learn what your client does when he's not talking with you.

Chapter 9.
Candidate Preparation For Interviews

Spending time with a candidate in preparation for the interview is one of the more natural and easier parts of your role as a recruiter. Encouraging, motivating, and dressing up a candidate is similar to what your mother did for you before sending you off to school or to your first prom. We've seen it done so many times before that it should be old hat for us. But there is no difference in what you do and what your mom did; your livelihood depends upon how well you prepare the candidate to present themselves professionally.

Preparing candidates does not mean programming them with artificial responses to textbook questions. It doesn't mean for them to misrepresent the facts and their qualifications to the employer. Nor does it mean giving a candidate answers to a clients questions that the candidate doesn't agree with and might forget later on.

Preparation means allowing the candidate to present the facts and history of their business accomplishments in the best possible light. And informing a candidate as to what a manager needs from a potential employee.

> Nothing in what you suggest to a candidate in preparing them should be construed by the candidate as manipulative or deceptive. The candidate will never trust you again and will inform the client as to your actions. If you feel the need to try and "program" a candidate for an interview; then it's the wrong candidate for the job. Period. Another point to consider is that no mature, intelligent, psychologically stable adult will withstand being programmed to do or say things that are unnatural or untrue under the pressure of an employment interview. We all resort to what comes naturally to us when under pressure. Like a person learning a new golf swing, the swing will feel uncomfortable for a while until it's been transferred into muscle memory. The candidate is no different than the golfer in that an unnatural statement will not hold up under pressure, without some kind of validation of belief or consistency of use. In other words; it won't work.

Seven keys to an offer.

Assuming the candidate you're sending on this interview has been pre-qualified up to this point as having interest and meets a client's qualifications, your prep work should be minimal. Here's a list of some key areas to review with the candidate. They should not be presented as "musts" because the candidate will take offense and feel forced into what you want. Present the ideas in a conversational fashion that encourages the candidate to reflect on the advice and its relevance to the situation; not just to your pocketbook.

1. Do the homework. Find out the five Ws relating to the company the candidate is interviewing with, the industry, the manager. Try and talk with a few people in the industry right now as well as someone who recently left it, asking why they left. The candidates willingness to invest their own time and energy are the serious ones willing to change jobs. They are the ones whom the manager will conclude are serious as well. Such preparation shows an energy level and a curiosity for life and work, which further impresses a potential employer. The candidates who ask you for the information and a zillion questions *could* be showing signs of a tree-hugger- one who says they want to make a change, but can't pull the trigger for some reason unless the risk is so minute that they could do it with their eyes closed. Are the candidate's questions of interest and opportunity, compared to risk avoidance in making a change?

2. More homework. Explore the culture, pace, stability and customers in the industry. Suggest that candidates envision themselves in the industry, day-in and day-out for a few years.

3. Check out the competition. What do they do similarly or differently compared to your client? Be prepared to talk with the hiring manager at length about his or her findings. Show the manager you know how to find information with little facts to start with.

4. Prepare the candidate's so that a candidate's strengths mesh with the important traits and skills in the industry. List accomplishments--both past and present--reflecting areas of interest to the manager and document diverse interests and

113

leadership abilities through both business avenues and volunteer organizations within their local community. A well-rounded individual shows an intelligence and reasonableness which can be hard to find in these days of a strong economy and high growth.

5. The counter-offer. Ask your candidate what will happen should your client extend an offer to them within the next ten days. What will their current employer do? Will the candidates be fired on the spot and escorted to the door? Will the candidate be offered a promotion and raise on the spot and persuaded to stay with the company? Review very carefully what a counter-offer will do to your candidate's career with that company; how blackmailing a boss to get what you want is not looked on too favorably when it comes to promotion time. Stress the reasons for leaving you were given when you first talked and make sure nothing has changed. (I suggest that you have your client ask the same question regarding a counter-offer to the candidate so the candidate feels everyone is acting in the candidate's best interest, and that it's not a ploy by you the recruiter, to guarantee you a fee.)

6. Prepare a list of critical questions for the interview with the hiring manager. Not too many, but enough to get a good feel for the company and the responsibilities of the job. Remind the candidate that the employer has the floor during the first interview and the candidate needs to sell his own abilities first, before interrogating the manager as to his qualifications and company profile. There's a place for this, but not on the first interview. Patience.

7. Remind the candidate to never discuss compensation on the first interview. Never, never, never. If you have qualified them well, you'll know that the money will be right, but this topic

should not be addressed prematurely. The candidate needs to create value in the managers' mind first. Make it impossible for the manager see anyone else in the job except your candidate. When this point is reached in the interview process, then it's time to talk dollars. Now you have leverage, not a moment before. Patience is a key to securing a great offer. Stress to the candidate the value of selling his or her ability first.

A lot of these ideas may appear obvious and simplistic, but I have found them to be misunderstood and ignored by a great majority of the interviewees out there. People still hold onto the advice their parents or friends gave them a million years ago but most tactics are outdated, irrelevant to certain markets and incompatible with what the goal might be in the interview. So please spend the time to prepare a candidate before a client meeting.

At the interview: Eight steps to an offer.

Once the candidate walks in the manager's door, your work is finished. You will be able to do nothing more to make an impact with the client related to your candidate. So prior to the interview, encourage the candidate to have an agenda to follow in the interview. Here's some ideas.

1. Have a goal or objective for the interview. The first goal should be to secure a second interview.
2. Have questions prepared if the interview pace slows down or the manager answers all your questions before you look at your notes.
3. Bring documentation. Have awards, letters, pictures, memos, anything showing you're someone special in your business. A neat, crisp, error-free resume is also mandatory.

4. Have a reference sheet available, but don't give it to the client unless they request it. If the client is unsure about a candidate's ability to learn the job, at this point it's okay to pull out the references and suggest they call.

5. Demonstrate enthusiasm for life and business. Don't badmouth your current employer regardless of how much you hate your boss or company. Be politically correct when giving sound reasons for leaving.

6. Convince the manager that you want the job and ask for the job, or another interview.

7. Follow-up. Send a thank you letter the same day if possible. Keep it short, simple, and upbeat.

8. Follow-up with a call to the manager within four days to restate interest in the job and see if you can schedule an interview at that time. Some employers don't like candidates to call them directly when they are working with a recruiter, but I have found if the candidate is in the running and I know it, there is no harm calling direct. Candidates can often do a better job selling themselves than I can.

Candidate debriefing

This debriefing is very similar to the client debriefing discussed previously. If the candidate is open and talkative about what went on in the interview, chances are it went well. If you have to draw things out of the candidate and lead them through the meeting with "what happened then?", then he or she probably won't be going back for another visit. Encourage the candidate to tell you what his or her feeling about the opportunity. Listen, take careful notes and ask open-ended questions to see whether the job was attractive or not. Ask if the candidate wants you to sell him or her further to the client. Does he want the job, and could he see himself working for the manager and the firm? Any major concerns? Would she accept an offer if one was given within the next ten days? Is their anything preventing her from starting immediately?

If the candidate appears mildly interested, speak with him the next day and take his pulse again. Sometimes he or she may get more excited after a night to think it over. Others will sometimes play hard to get. If so, you'll need to let them know of other candidates in the running and ask if you should sell them hard to the hiring manager. **The sooner you can demonstrate to the candidate that you will win regardless of who the client hires, you'll be able to gain the trust of the candidate.** When you become a cheerleader and coach for him or her, instead of forcing the candidate to make a decision, he or she will confide in you and ask your help. Here's a few sentences I use to demonstrate this strategy:

" John, I feel it's important to tell you that, from a pure business perspective, it doesn't matter to me which candidate of mine my client hires. Either way I'm going to get paid, so I don't want you to think I'm forcing you to make a decision you don't want to make. If you are genuinely interested in this opportunity, then tell me so and I'll promote your enthusiasm to the client as hard as I can. If not, then let's pass on this one and move on. Fair enough? What would you like me to do?"

This approach has flushed out the truly interested and saved me tons of time spinning my wheels with candidates only interested in getting interview practice. It is a clean and effective way to demonstrate a professional impression to a candidate.

Early in my recruiting career I tried to force a candidate to take an interview because I felt it was a great job. Now I realize that if the candidate doesn't see the opportunity as a solid one, then that person's not the right candidate for the job.

117

The less you sell an opportunity to someone, the more trust you develop for the next time. I look at my job as kind of a "shoulder tapper." I'm the one who says, " You know, I just found out about a neat opportunity. Would you like to hear more about it? I think it could be a tremendous move for someone." This approach has whetted the appetite of more candidates than any other approach I have used. I think it works so well because I'm not selling, I'm expressing, I'm experiencing a wondering to the candidate and they get caught up in the event, too.

If the candidate has gone through two or three interviews, you're getting to the offer stage. Client and candidate are ready to pull the trigger and you need to set up a target to shoot at. Let's look at the strategies to use in the next chapter.

Chapter 10.
Negotiating The Offer For The Candidate

Here's the part of the recruiting process where you earn your money. And sometimes earn even more through effective negotiating on the client's and candidate's behalf.

Up to this point the progression of excitement and anticipation on the candidate's part should be high. The candidate has been doing the work of interviewing, researching, sending letters, getting feedback and guidance from you on positioning himself to address the right topics and career highlights, so an offer should be expected and he should be eager to accept. Right? Well....let's make sure it goes together. This is where a lot of deals can fall apart by not qualifying and dealing with the sensitive issues and assumptions of both the candidate and the client.

For example; here's some general viewpoints that each party in this situation can take.

Client
-Thinks her company is great and people should be glad they're getting an offer from them.
-Feels the offer she has have in mind is fair-regardless of the candidate's current earnings.
-Is confident she can make the offer personally without your interjection of ideas and observations.
-Has a natural suspicion of the recruiter and thinks you'll jack up the salary requirements of your candidate to get a bigger fee. (Not a bad idea. Why didn't I think of that?)

Candidate

-Has been told since the dawn of time to never except the first offer. Always test it.

-Sees risk in making a change even though he wants out of his current job, big time.

-Wants to know what the offer is up-front, from you.

-Naturally suspicious of recruiters because we make big bucks if candidate takes the job. Who cares if it is right for them or not, they'll reason.

- Thinks he's worth top salary and bonus plan, even without industry experience.

Recruiter

-Knows more about the candidate's expectations than the client.

- Knows more about the client's opportunity than the candidate.

- Understands the process and strategy to make it work.

- Deals in the courtship ritual of career changes everyday.

-Likes to make the offer to the candidate. Does a better job.

All of these viewpoints are valid and reasonable to expect given their respective roles in the scenario. So how do you coordinate all these feelings, egos and assumptions to make an offer go together? There is no one answer. Too bad for you and me. However, I have some strategies which will increase your placement ratio tremendously. Let's first discuss the *candidate* relationship.

The counter-offer sermon

If you have been following the search process so far, you have:

1. Been taking the candidate's temperature over the past weeks to verify his continued interest in securing an offer and employment with this company. He should be committed and ready to accept the offer you have discussed.

2. You've reviewed and related back to him the reasons he is are making a change, **other than for money** although a better compensation plan is expected. I suggest you prepare the candidate to accept an offer which is on the **low** side of the offer range. In this way you're assured the candidate will accept the job at the lower figure, and should the client listen to you and offer on the **high** side, then the candidate will feel relieved and happy when the larger offer comes in. The worst case scenario is that the client comes in at the lower number and the candidate feels that your advice was sound and that he made the right decision. Mirror back to him from your notes what he told you earlier in your first dialogues with him. He should be nodding yes at this point.

3. You've discussed with him the time and energy he's invested to this point, and any feeling of backing out is purely nerves and first night jitters. It's nothing to be surprised about and is expected. Stress the fact that if it weren't right he would have felt this nervousness sooner and quit the process long ago.

4. You've had a conversation with the candidate relating the client's sincere belief that he is the best person for the position right now. The client has interviewed numerous individuals and this candidate has risen to the top of the mountain and is proclaimed the winner and new champion.

5. Cover the counter-offer from the candidate's current employer with the candidate <u>now</u> to avoid looking like a money-hungry recruiter after the counter-offer comes. The candidate needs to understand the career suicide of accepting a counter-offer once he's resigned. Have the client spend time discussing this issue as well. This way the candiate feels his best interest is being looked out for, and the new company

knows what's goes on. Covering the counter-offer at this point also helps put the candidate in the mindset of resigning and starting a new career. The transition will not be as difficult if he goes into the offer/acceptance period knowing he will be quitting soon.

With the client, you should:
1. Confirm the salary and other bonuses, commissions, benefits and whatever else is part of the package. No surprises are allowed at this point. Are the offer numbers she has in line with what your candidate is expecting? If not, call time-out and regroup with your candidate.
2. Position the client to extend an offer on the high side of what she feels would be satisfactory to secure the candidate's acceptance. Better to come in a little high with an offer, than embarrass the company with a low number and have the candidate say" adios." In a strong economy, the candidate will have a slight edge, because the pool of strong candidates is less than in a slower market. Thus, the candidate could have more offers to consider and be willing to negotiate more strongly and take the chance of losing the job. Educate your client of this fact if it applies.
3. Suggest that *you* extend the offer, since the candidate knows you better.You can eliminate at lot of the bitterness that can develop between the manager and employee as the negotiations go on. With the recruiter as the go-between, it saves reputations and bad feelings if one party is not as willing to budge on certain issues. Plus, the recruiter can make the offer in an enthusiastic manner without showing the overanxiousness a manager may show. The recruiter also sees benefits and opportunities which are routine to a manager and not always enthusiastically presented

4. Review the time the client will give the candidate to accept. I suggest giving 24 hours, with a specific time the next day to decide or the offer is null and void. if the candidate has been truly interested and committed to securing a job with your client, he has already made the decision to accept--long before the official offer comes across. It reduces the chances of the candidate getting cold feet and submitting to advice by those tree-huggers and tire kicker friends and family members. **It also protects you from losing the #2 candidate (if you're fortunate enough to have the #2) in the dust should #1 not accept. You can keep him or her alive and stall with the final decision until #1 candidate accepts within that 24 hour period.**

The waiting game

Arrange for the candidate to call you right after he meets or talks with the client to receive an offer. Same goes with the client; have her call you to review the details and final numbers.

The candidate should sound excited, relieved, numb, in shock-- and certainly *not* disappointed. If the meeting went as planned, celebrate! Congratulate the candidate on making an educated and mature decision. Encourage him to share his good news soon with friends and family members. (This approach encourages the person to stand by the decision even when fear and "buyer's remorse" sets in the day before he resigns. We all know it's embarrassing to go and tell others we changed our mind or made a poor decision. Telling friends and family helps seal the event.)

If you hear less than positive feedback, review carefully what was relayed and discussed. Look for surprises and changes you didn't anticipate. If there are details still to be worked out, keep the talk positive and optimistic. Ask the candidate what he wants you to do. Relate your feelings and observations about the situation and tell him you'll call him back if there is a problem you need to address. Is it money, relocation, benefits, commission, vacation, the training program-or lack of one, a start date too soon or too late, or that a non-compete contract, drug test or physical is required? Note anything that he shares with you and speak with the manager immediately.

In discussing these issues with the client make sure the objections are clear and consistent. Look for misunderstandings of terms and expectations. Identify what issues are adjustable and which are cut in stone. Verify that the manager wants it to work and wants to secure the candidate for employment. If yes, educate her to the reasoning behind your candidate's request and observations. Suggest she puts herself in the candidate's shoes to see why your candidate feels the way he does. In most cases the client will see the points you make and make concessions to accommodate the candidate, as long as the requests are not far off of the initial expectations discussed between both client and candidate.

Cold feet

Which brings up a good point. If the candidate changes the rules of the game after the offer, i.e., changes the salary level he'd accept, increases the signing bonus, wants or extends the start date past the two weeks standard, nip this in the bud quickly by stating to the candidate what you had agreed upon and determine exactly his goal is in making these new requests.

Don't be afraid to tell the candidate you willing to pull him from the offer stage right now if you feel your your client is being used to secure a better offer at the candidate's current company, or that the candidate is unsure about making a career move right now. Your time and reputation with the client is too valuable to be diseased by a candidate who changes the rules after the game has begun. Walk away from the candidate and suggest to the client that you feel the candidate is demonstrating behavior that may show signs of immaturity and an unwillingness to commit one hundred percent. Suggest to the client that they proceed with the #2 candidate who may want the job more that #1 and will do a great job as well.

Finishing touches

Now that the offer has come together, here's the checklist to follow in the days and weeks until the candidate's start date.
1. Get the client to put a written offer in the mail ASAP. everything related to the hiring decision including the insurance information, benefits booklet, pictures, training agenda--you name it--it should be sent.
 2. Arrange for the candidate to write an acceptance letter ASAP. This helps insure the candidate will stay with his decision and not get cold feet. It also guarantees the company will hire and pay him should a hiring freeze occur right after he is offered the job. It also shows the conviction of the candidate to work for the manager.
3. Review how and when the candidate will resign. Walk him through the process of giving two weeks notice and not burning bridges by badmouthing his current employer. Give him one main reason for resigning, such as lack of growth, desire to work for a bigger company or a higher earning

potential, and leave it at that. Tell him not to accept any "let's go out to lunch to discuss it further" ploys. He should simply state his peace, wrap up loose ends and say goodbye.

4. Have the candidate call the client right after resigning and keep her informed of the exact start date. If it's longer than two weeks, arrange to have the client have breakfast or lunch before the start date to keep warm fuzzies and the commitment strong. This in-between jobs time is the most vulnerable time for the candidate. It's kind of like a "man (or women) without a country" syndrome. The recruiter should also stay in touch.

5. Have the client send a simple gift or flowers to the candidate's spouse welcoming him or her to the new organization. It makes the spouse feel a part of the process and reinforces that the candidate made the right choice by going with such a thoughtful manager and company.

6. Check in with the client and candidate a week or so after the start date to see if everything is as expected. Carefully address issues to make sure no one feels offended that you're still involved.

7. Ask the client for more business! Ride the wave!

8. Don't forget to send the client a bill--a big one.

Here's a copy of a checklist I give to my clients to assist them in covering all the bases of bringing on a new employee. For most managers, hiring new people takes a small percentage of their time so they aren't as familiar with the details that should be covered. This list is a welcome outline for many managers who are busy enough as it is.

My friends Carl Podlasek and Pete Rickerson gave me a copy and I've modified it over the years. Give a copy to your client.

CHECKLIST FOR NEW EMPLOYEE

Driving record_____
Any non-compete or disclosure agreements to
sign_____
Salary and bonus plans. Review dates
discussed_____
W2 forms and payroll information_____
Health and medical information_____
Benefits information/vacation policy_____
Physical and/or drug screen_____
Orientation schedule_____
Announcement- In house, trade journals,
newspapers_____
Business cards ordered/enroll in business associations
Flowers to spouse_____
Congratulatory letter_____
Company car in order, if applicable_____
Company credit cards issued_____
Car phone, pager, fax machine, laptop_____
Photo_____
Travel profile to travel agent and frequent flyer mile program
sign-up_____

Act like a four-year old. Notice how much information a child gets from you when asking "WHY?" to everything you do?

Chapter 11.
Negotiating Your Fee. Twelve Creative Ways To *Keep* More Of What You Earn.

Recruiter at the butcher shop: How much is your ground sirloin?
Butcher: $1.69 a pound.
Recruiter: A $1.69 a pound?! Man that's high. The butcher down the street sells it for $1.29 a pound.
Butcher: Then go buy it from him.
Recruiter: He's sold out.
Butcher: ...Funny, when I'm sold out, I sell it for $1.19 a pound!

Bottom line: everybody wants a deal. And managers with recruiting budgets are no different.

Fee negotiating is a topic that everybody has a strong opinion on and rather than give you some hard and fast rules to live by, I'd rather give you some new and creative ways to negotiate your fees without giving away the store.

> *The ability to negotiate the best fee possible is the easiest way to earn more money without working any harder and it allows you to work with the best companies in the market because they want the best too!*

Remember: I am not talking about negotiating with the manager who doesn't work with recruiters. These folks will lure you into working with them for a low fee because they say they can't afford the high fee. So because you have a big heart and want to prove to them you can do it, you lower your fee and start the search, only to be frustrated when it comes time to make an offer, because *their* boss finally realizes how much it's gonna cost, puts the cabash on the deal and runs an ad in the paper. "Sorry" is what you hear and you move on. **Moral: Spend your time and energy negotiating with fee paying companies. You're chances improve immediately because of their history of paying a fee.**

I decided to dedicate a whole section to fee negotiating because of the many facets of the process. It's important to have ammunition in the event of a lucrative search opportunity.

Excuses, excuses.

There is no way to avoid negotiating fees. The situation will come up every time in some shape or form and you have to deal with it. Taking a hard line position such as: "Take my fee agreement or leave it" will land you little business, so you need ways to be firm, yet be a little flexible to appease the other party. I don't like the process either, but the money and life of a recruiter is still the best job out there for me.

A few noteworthy ideas to keep in mind as we get into this topic.

A. The bigger the fee, the easier the search.

B. A manager with a tight wallet on fees will have a tight wallet in offers to candidates. They go hand in hand.

C. Extended guarantees beyond thirty days are dangerous to your wallet. You're a recruiter, not an insurance company for the manager's decisions. Consider a "replacement only guarantee" if a potentially good customer wants a longer guarantee.

D. When you hear the phrase "Just send me the candidates, we'll talk about the fee later," you should reply "no can do." Get the fee agreed upon *now* rather than later. You'll get sucked in to giving away the store if the client likes a person and makes you feel like you'll blow the deal if you don't give in. It's called **"Candidate kidnapping"**: the client interviews the candidate and wants to hire him. **Voila! Kidnapped** . And you pay the ransom; or the reduced fee. Bottom line: If they won't agree to a fee, walk away.

E. Work as hard as you can to follow your written fee agreement to the letter. You will be respected by the manager for your conviction to your policy and belief in your abilities. If you try to make points by folding up like a wimp because the potential manager chewed you down in price, you both lose. You may not get the business right away, but in time the manager will come back to you and pay your fee when they've become frustrated with the "deal givers, but no results" recruiters. **Remember: you work just as hard on a small fee as you do a big one. It's the same process and requires the same energy.**

Yeah but.....

You may hear comments like these from prospective hiring managers:

- Your competition out there is only charging a 20% fee. Why is yours so much higher? Your potential response: My fee is the standard rate charged by professional recruiters. I can discount the fee, but please tell me what part of my search work I can eliminate to allow the fee to be reduced. Do you discount the price of your product or service by nearly 30% for your customers? (In our business, 30% is the *true* discount of the fee when going from the maximum of 30% down to 20%.)

- We will only pay a flat fee of $5,000, but we pay within ten days. Your response: That's OK, I'll wait another ten days or so for the money, charge the competitive rate and not sacrifice my work towards filling your search quickly.

- We're a small company and don't have that big a budget to pay your high fees. Your response: That is exactly why you need me; to help grow your business. Is the cost of hiring a person who will make you money, worth less than not having the business at all? If you're hiring a salesperson, one sale made could cover the cost of the search. I encourage you to interview three candidates whom I have identified, and then interview three candidates from your own sources. If my candidates ares better than it behooves you to invest in the better of the two. It's cheaper to pay for value once, than to make excuses for poor decisions forever.

- We pay a smaller fee, but we will have a ton of openings, so you'll make it up in volume. Your response: Do you have a turnover problem? Why so many openings? I'm interested in one successful search at a time. I can give a volume discount, but only after we have filled the numerous openings you speak of.

Rule to live by: Discount fees *after* you have successfully completed many searches. Promises of multiple openings are, in most cases sincere, but can fall short of the numbers you're promised.

I don't feel the urge to spend a lot of time trying to convince managers to use my services. I trust in the history of the profession that the managers will come back to those with the track record of achievement in recruiting. To continue discounting and justifying my fee against those who lower their price because they need the business or are desperate is crazy. Realize that you are as good as the next recruiter and your fee is payment for making their company money!

Oh, But I must Try and Convince Them to Use My Services!

If you are compelled to try and convince a non-user of recruiters to consider your services, here's a formula to walk the manager through to allow him or her to see how much money they could be losing by not hiring a new person quickly. And of course, you have the ability to find that person more quickly than any method that hiring manager has.

Here's an example of a vacancy in an outside sales territory where you can really see how the value is mistaken in *assumed* costs.

Average territory $500,000 in yearly sales divided per month = $41,666.66. If a position is open three months then it's $41,666.66 X 3 = $125,000 in sales that could be lost without a sales person covering the territory. The fee you charge is small potatoes compared to losing over 100K in sales. And even if half of the sales are still retained, the fee still looks like a bargain and a smart move for the manager to make in getting you started. Let the client see they lose more than they spend. And they only have to spend it if they hire your candidate--not before!

Always be looking ahead to where your next business is coming from. Ask yourself on a regular basis,"If every job order I'm working on right now disappears, where is my next placement?" If you think along these lines, you will always be in touch with new business marketing.

Consider this fact: If you find a salesperson for a plastic bottle company and that person sells a million dollars worth of them in the first year, the corporation's profit margin-even at a conservative 5%-amounts to a $50,000 profit! Is your fee worth paying to secure this kind of profit? And you haven't even factored in the interest they make on the money, and the fact they're able to keep the plant running and workers employed. And the manager's bonus comes out of working capital. So justifying your fee is a lot simpler than you think. *Have these formulas written down so you're able to addresss the points when a manager looks at the short-sided view of what you can do for them.*

Hiring managers sometimes have a hard time getting fees approved because it involves the chance that they may be wrong, embarassed *and* pay a fee. If the candidate doesn't work out, then the fee and the search are history and they need to start over and answer to the boss on what went wrong. And the world of recruiting and hiring is an inexact science.

You can see how it can be easier for a manager to rationalize the low sales volume in a vacant territory while the hiring manager looks for the perfect candidate, than to justify a search that may not produce results. Your goal is to give the manager courage and information to conduct a serious search using your expertise to find someone to create sales or improve customer service, or revitalize the plant. Create an atmosphere of energy and growth in using your services, not a big invoice that they need to sweat out with the boss. If your candidate is better than the one they have identified, they'll see the difference and pay the fee gladly.

Secret formulas for creative fee negotiations

Here's a collection of innovative and clever ways to structure your fee agreements when a client insists on some kind of a discount. Some you may be familiar with, others may surprise and enthuse you. Keep in mind the power of words, numbers and percentages. For example: A "decade" sounds longer than "ten years"; a 10% discount could sound better than a reduction of $600 in the fee; *a guarantee* is better than a *promise;* an *agreement* is less intimidating than a *contract.* When negotiating with potential clients, be aware of how they view their business and use words and pictures they can relate to.

Many of us are too quick to discount our fee from a standard 30% to 25% if you're in the permanent placement side of recruiting. It's only a simple 5% discount, right? Wrong! The true discount is about 18%. Let me show you.
Example:
 Salary $100,000 30% fee= $30,000
 Salary $100,00,00 25% fee= $25,000
The difference of $5,000 is about an 18% discount, not 5%.

Because of the simplicity of dropping 30% to 25%, we can get stuck giving away a big chunk of money without having too.

Many of these fee options are not familiar to managers, so practice patience when explaining them and stress the benefits of creative arrangements.

Option 1. Standard rates are a maximum 30% fee. Period. You run the show your way. This is a great stand to take if you anticipate the manager or company to be difficult to work with. If your opinion turns out to be true, you'll still make money despite the difficulties.

Option 2. First hire 30%. Second hire 25%. Third hire 20%. This is pretty basic and easy to remember, AND easy to see how much money *you're* losing.

Option 3. First, second and third placement--at full fee. Third, fourth and fifth hire at 25% fee. Sixth seventh and eight hire at 20% fee. Not a bad way to structure it if the searches are easier to fill and you won't need to do extensive recruiting or reinvent the wheel.

Option 4. A flat fee reflecting a reduced fee based on projected first year earnings. This is a popular approach because everybody knows what the charge will be from the start--no questions asked. The problem can be that this fee can stay at this amount for years and you'll be skeptical of approaching the client to increase it. You may want to find a way to convert that flat fee into some kind of a percentage amount. That way inflation will take care of keeping the fee in line with rising costs and salaries. Or build in a yearly cost of living increase to the flat fee. **The bottom line is: don't get locked into a number for life.**

Option 5. Engagement fee, 25% of estimated fee paid upfront, non-refundable, to insure commitment on the client's part that the search is for real and urgent. This tactic works well in a strong economy where candidates are scarce. It tells the client that you're serious in wanting to work with them, but need their commitment to the project so your recruiting costs are covered, should they change their minds and not fill the opening. Point out to the client that all your costs are incurred at the beginning of the search, so to insure against any losses, the engagement fee protects this. I will consider discounting the fee slightly if a company is willing to give me an engagement fee. The odds go up to fill the search when they have already invested dollars with me already. (Engagement fee is also an excellent way to nurse your client into future retainer business. They will see that it doesn't even hurt!)

Option 6. Base fee on cumulative salaries of hires. Example:
-0-$100,000 of salary dollars--30% fee
-101,000-$200,000 salary dollars--25% fee

- 201,000-$250,000 salary dollars--20% fee
-Start back at 30% when you reach
$250,000.

This is a great way to lock in a client to long-term savings and to building a relationship with you. A win/win all around. You can adjust the ranges of salary discounting to fit your industry pay scale, and maybe set it up to provide aproximately three hires in the first group and three in the next.

Option 7. Sign a national agreement in-return for a reduced fee. Note I didn't say contract, but agreement. It's less committment for the client, yet it creates a synergy and understanding that will go a long way. Do indeed sign a contract if you can, guaranteeing the client uses only you and pays your fee. But if you have not done a lot of business with them yet, it might be hard to get this signed. Be patient and keep performing above and beyond the call--a contract will come.

Option 8. Run an ad. They pay and you collect resumes and screen candidates. In-turn you reduce your fee and keep additional leads and candidates generated from the ad. This is a good way to source some additional candidates, but it can be time consuming and downright depressing getting numerous calls from those seeking a change without the qualifications or preparation. I don't do these too often, unless business is in the dumps.

Option 9. Regular fee agreement- a 10% discount off that amount. Clean and simple.

Option 10. Reduce fee slightly if paid in ten days. A 2% net 10 is textbook discounting in business. It's worth a try.

Option 11. Avoid extended guarantees. If you need to comply, consider a 50% refund after 60 days, for example, rather than the full amount. Or pro-rate the refund over the length of the guarantee. Remember: You're a recruiter, not an insurance company.

Option 12. Get a retainer. These are easier to contract than you may think. The only difference between a contingent fee search and a retained search is the method of payment, not the method of search. The full-time retainer firms attempt to paint a mystical picture of how they seek out and secure talent for client companies, however the approach is not much different. I do retained searches with companies I have worked with in the past or if I have a good understanding of their business. A retainer can be great , but if the company is unsure of their needs you can be sucked dry of time and energy seeking out a candidate that doesn't exist. Use caution when accepting a retainer search. If you primarily do contingent work you have the option of walking away from a contingent search. It's a little tougher when you have a retainer contract that needs to be fulfilled.

If the fee gets too low, walk away and find a better one. Low fees are a pain and the managers expect miracles. Stand firm , they will come back to you when they've frustrated themselves with cheap fixes and poor quality candidates.

Closing thoughts on fee negotiation

Try not to accept any offer of fee reductions on the spot. Think it over for a day and then respond. Most people,managers included, don't like giving a "take it or leave it offer." So calling the next day and renegotiating the deal

139

may earn you a bigger fee and better terms. You may gain some better ideas on creating a better agreement by sleeping on it. The manager will also respect you for the time you've taken to make the decision. It demonstrates you're not desperate for the work and shows you're a true professional. Remember: They have pressures too to get the position filled. They may be praying you'll take the search.

If you follow some of these tactics on a regular basis you'll earn more money and retain more clients long-term, even though your fees might be higher than your so-called competition.

> **The difference in being an average biller and being in the elite Top 5% in the nation is not more placements. It's getting paid what you earned on the ones you did place. Always test the fee a client proposes to you. If it's fair, do it. If not, walk away.**

Chapter 12.
Positioning Yourself As An Expert.

Sell the Thunder, They'll Buy the Rain.

The dictionary defines expert as," special skill or knowledge." And as a full-time recruiter for any reasonable length of time, you indeed become an expert in the field of recruiting. It doesn't mean you'll be right all the time, but you understand the progressive steps it takes to secure the best fit for a candidate and company in a reasonable time period.

This business of professional recruiting is the ultimate in networking. Without the ability and willingness to gather names, contacts, information, history or you-name-it, a person will never really experience the true potential for gratification of mind, heart and bank account in this business. And this networking ritual you engage in everyday is where your expertise comes from. Consider the fact that in one week you are in contact with more people aggressively looking for a new job than *any* manager you will ever work with. How could these managers have a greater understanding for market conditions, pressures on a candidate to make a career change, or a thorough understanding of what compensation plans are in place today in that manager's industry? They can't know more than you in these subject areas! See how you are now the expert?

The good news is yes, you are an expert. The bad news is the hiring manager still won't believe you all the time. You need to position yourself so that they see their learning from you as a natural part of the business transaction.

Thinking On Your Seat focuses on the behavioral approach to recruiting; positioning the information you convey in the form of a question to the candidate or client, or in a,"What do you think about this?" approach. And this process starts the first moment you spoke with that person.

✳ Recruiting is built upon the strength of referrals, all from people willing to share ideas with you. The fact that you get this information is a credit to you because it's a sign of trust. A sign that people feel you're worth staying in contact with to help them. Selfish as it may seem at times, it's still flattering to know you are respected and needed in more ways than one.

Seven steps to becoming an expert

So how do you become an expert in the recruiting industry, you ask? Here are a few suggestions to help you remain in contact with employers and demonstrate to them that you're in touch with today's market and committed to recruiting for the long term.

1. Regular contact. Maintain a rigorous schedule of contacting client companies. This may mean every month for some, every six months for others. It depends upon how your industry functions. "Out of sight out of mind" is true in this business. Remember the story of the manager who forgot the recruiter had called him three weeks ago in an earlier chapter? He didn't want to remember in the first place. Call to say "hello" and remind them you are still in the business and would like to work with them. Ask questions related to the type of people you search for and plant seeds in their minds of where their

next vacancies could be. Ask about promotions, retirements, poor performers, territory realignments, anything to get them thinking about the need to use you. **Remember: Learn what that manager does when he's not talking to you.**

2. Send them copies of any article you see related to their business, their hobbies, hometowns, favorite sports teams, or performers etc. Send them information you receive on training, seminars for business people, investment information and things that you find interesting and informative. For example, I'm a big *Far Side* fan. I have a daily calendar of *Far Side* humor and use the pages to send notes to clients which I know have a crazy view of the world, like I do. They love it and send me back even better ones.

3. Send them copies of articles you have written. The best way to gain recognition as an expert in your field is to be published in one of the trade journals or magazines in your marketplace. These publications are always looking for someone with a good idea or interesting observation about the industry. If you're not a competent writer hire someone to assist you and get the piece in print! The cost to pay a professional writer is well worth it, if clients call you with their business or to seek your opinion.

4. You gotta eat, don't you? Go out and chow down with a potential client or current one. Engage in the art of conversation. Have breakfast, lunch or dinner once in a while and relax. Take them to a ball game, roller derby, political debate, whatever. If you truly enjoy their company--call them. If you don't like them personally, but respect them as business people and fellow human beings you don't need to spend social time with them; just give them great service and they'll be loyal to you forever. I have a number of clients that have no desire

to socialize with me or any other recruiter for that matter. They keep business and social relationships very separate. And that's OK. It takes the pressure off both of us from not having to fake a relationship to gain business or remain in good standing.

5. Call clients once in a while and present a superstar; someone whom you have met that you feel is special and would be a great asset to any company. Your clients will appreciate you thinking of them and may even hire the individual.

6. Be polite and brief. I know I can get a little wordy at times on the phone, so I have to really concentrate on getting to the purpose of my call and signing off without too much blabber. Show a respect for managers time and encourage them to call you when there is a trace of a search in the air. Stress to them you work in total confidence and giving you advance notice of a search will improve the timeliness and quality of the candidate without a lot of down time in their open position or territory.

7. Always send clients new business cards (2 always), newsletters, brochures, change of address cards, anything you can to stay in contact.

Become an expert in the *candidate's* eyes too!

The same ideas and strategies apply to working with candidates as with the client. There are only a few variations on the theme.

1. Stay in touch with solid candidates on a regular basis, particularly the ones who refer the most and best people to you. They are worth their weight in gold.
2. Always send thank-you notes to candidates after you meet with them, speak on the phone, or if they refer someone to you. A note of thanks is so simple yet people still do not use this effective and proper etiquette approach in business. Don't you remember the last person to send you a thank you note?
3. Periodically send out notes, articles, or pamphlets on topics involving career change, new markets to investigate, or how to get a raise. These pieces not only keep you in contact with candidates, but stimulates candidates to make the change they've been contemplating for some time. You can be the catalyst for their movement to a better opportunity.

Positioning yourself as an expert is really nothing more than performing your job as a recruiter in the most effective manner you can. Demonstrating commitment through your words and actions proves to the people in your marketplace that you're here to stay, and they'll stay in touch with you to seek your counsel and assistance.

If a situation has to be forced with a prospect, it's not right. There is a certain rhythm to a search that you can feel. Strive to get to that point.

Chapter 13.
Visualization and Brainstorming for Profit

Seeing the placement in your mind's eye

Visualization is the process of placing your mind in a concentrated state to focus on a specific event you wish to occur.

For example, have you ever had the experience when you were thinking of someone and the next minute that person calls you on the phone? Or you're in your car driving down the road and think of someone and you look over and that person is in the car next to you. We have all had these experiences many times, yet we push these events off as coincidence. I personally don't believe in coincidences. I believe, along with many other psychologists, behaviorists, and theologists that we create these occurrences with the power of our minds. That we actually are able to tune in to another person's mental energy field and transmit thoughts to them. Dr. Wayne Dyer calls this "synchronicity." My wife calls me haunted!

If you believe in this viewpoint or have had similar experiences, then you will enjoy the recruiting business thoroughly because you can harness and utilize this mental energy to your advantage. By spending time concentrating on persons who fit a profile, you can attract these individuals to you through other people or through direct contact. In other words, what you think manifests into reality. If you sincerely believe this, it will be of benefit to you. Here's how to begin.

1. Spend time writing out the profile of the person you need in a particular search you're involved with. Really concentrate on the qualities and characteristics this person needs to have to perform this job effectively.

2. In a quiet place at home or with your office door closed, close your eyes, breathe deeply and relax.

3. Allow your mind to wander around the faces and names of people you know in your life and picture them talking to their friends about the job you're looking to fill. See those persons appearing interested in the position and trying to find a way to call you on the phone or send you a resume. Don't force the process, just let these thoughts and feelings happen.

4. After about fifteen minutes, open your eyes, have a good stretch and go back to your daily business.

You won't be surprised when a call here or there comes in from a person who fits the profile you need. Or a candidate from the past calls you out-of-the-blue to say he or she is back in the market. I have had persons call me the day after I spent time visualizing, that I hadn't thought of in over a year. They said something made them think of me and call. This is fascinating stuff to explore! I have thought of contacts, ideas for securing more business, ideas for new writing projects, all from concentrating on what is important at that moment in time. That is what visualization is all about.

The art of visualization for recruiting is no different from any professional or amateur athlete who visualizes a good shot in golf, or making a free throw, or kicking a field goal. It's the same concept of energy transferred to thought and vice versa. Only we're using it to seek out a person who fits our goal of experience.

I encourage you to practice this exercise a number of times and not to give up on the power it can have. I was a bit skeptical to even discuss it in this manuscript for fear of ridicule, but I truly believe in the concept and know it is a big part of my and other people's success in our business. For more information and techniques to help you improve your skill in visualization, get your hands on the books written by Denis Waitley, such as *Psychology of Winning* or Dr. Wayne Dyer's book, *You'll See It When You Believe it.* Both are very popular personal development writers and do a great job honing the process of visualization to a fine degree.

If you're not mentally exhausted at the end of the day, one of two things may have occured: you didn't ask enough questions, or you made a placement before ten o'clock!

Chapter 14.
Managing Your Thoughts and Your Time to Increase Placements

There are hundreds of time management seminars given daily in this country. They are probably all pretty similar and cover the basics thoroughly, so I won't even try to educate you on the dozens of tactics and approaches to managing your time. But I would like to share some things I've learned from the top billers in the recruiting profession, as it relates to activities in this business.

Times a wastin', here's the ideas. Eight tips to efficient days--and no nights

1. Do the challenging part of our job at your peak energy times. Procrastination is the killer of any dream or significant goal, so fight the urge to postpone and do it now. Discipline is a word that I have heard a lot from top billers. A willingness to do the things you know you need to do, but don't necessarily like doing; It's part of the game. Plan your day around your peak energy times and work the system. My daily routine for example, revolves around two peak time windows 9am to 12pm, and 1pm- 3:30pm. Here's an example of how I like to layout my day.

8:00-9:00am: Check voice mail, faxes, messages, office events and review scheduled visitors and candidates. I fill my water glass.

9:00- Noon: Prospecting calls, recruiting calls, presenting candidate backgrounds to clients, and visits to client companies or potential clients.

Noon-1pm: Light lunch or maybe a healthclub visit or a run.

1-3pm: personal interviews with candidates and more prospecting and recruiting calls.

3-5pm: Return non-urgent calls, letter writing, scan publications of importance to a particular search, "rip and read" articles from trade journals and newspapers. Plan the next day.

Evenings: Relax, exercise, time with family/friends, chores, and reading/writing, both pleasure and business related. Visualization practice.

If I can stick to this regimen, within reason, I can accomplish most of what I need to do in a day.

2. "Formula fit" candidate calls take priority. We talked about the candidates whom you work with that fit a formula which your clients always look at first. When I find these individuals I drop what I'm doing and arrange to meet or speak further with them. They are my lifeline to business and I want to keep the rope fresh and strong. The rest of the non-formula fit candidates I call back after three o'clock.

3. Fight the urge to get up and wander. If I go home at the end of the day and my back is stiff and my rear is sore, then I know I've worked effectively that day. **The ear-to-rear ratio is critical to success in recruiting. Every successful recruiter I know spends most of their time with a phone to their ear while sitting on their rear. It all adds up to placements.** Phone time is money. At work, have fun,but work. When at home, play and recharge your battery. Sure, it is important to get up and stretch to get the blood flowing in

the limbs when you're at the office, but get up for *physical* reasons, not because you're bored or frustrated. Discipline yourself to make the effort necessary for success. The better you get at managing your time, the less time you'll spend sitting at your desk because you'll have free time. You'll spend more time out of the office visiting clients, securing more business. A new person in this business needs to establish a foundation of contacts and work habits to insure long lasting success. Sales trainer and speaker Tom Hopkins says it best, "Do the most productive thing at any given moment."

4. Be stingy with your time. Watch out for energy zappers like job hoppers, tirekickers, tree-huggers, curiosity seekers, long-time unemployed candidates, relatives, drop-ins and charity cases. These are people you probably can't place because your client looks for the top 10% in the field and a special background. Individuals in the group above don't fit your formula and chances are they don't socialize with a large number of those who fit your formula. So be nice and cordial, but say no to personal visits and extended phone calls. It is tough to be firm like this, but your job and commitment to your family necessitate a firm stand on protecting your time to work effectively.

5. Calculate your hourly and yearly income. To earn $52,000 a year, your hourly rate in a 40-hour work week is $25/hr. $100K a year would be $50/hr. **Ask yourself if you're performing tasks that will earn you this income**. If you're doing filing, or administrative functions for some reason and there is a way to pay someone less to do it, then hire someone and spend time on $50/hr tasks. This mindset is one of the best ways I know to keep focused on the art of working smart, *Thinking On Your Seat!*

6. Fight the temptation to take every call right at that moment. If you're in the middle of a project, a thought, a letter--call them back. People understand if you're busy, even hiring managers. It shows you actually work for a living too! Don't take a call if you're not prepared.

7. Do a time log for a week. See where you spend the majority of time and verify that it's where you want to be. Connected conversation earns more income than organizing your files and doing research. If you're spending more time doing paperwork and straightening your desk--burn your desk, and sit on the floor and call people!

8. Lay out your desk to have as many of the items you need to do your job within four feet. Here's an aerial shot of a efficient recruiters desk, which we saw in an earlier chapter as well. This picture shows how the files and forms and follow-up stuff is right at the finger tips. No wasted time and effort to find and send letters, notes, and brochures.

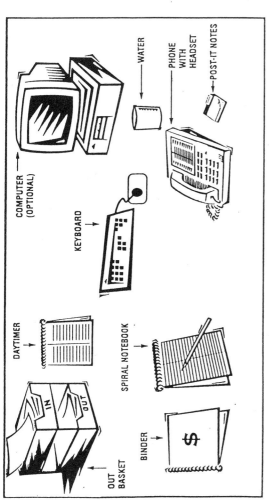

AERIAL VIEW OF AN EFFICIENT RECRUITERS DESK

COMPUTER
(OPTIONAL)

WATER

PHONE
WITH
HEADSET

POST-IT NOTES

KEYBOARD

DAYTIMER

SPIRAL NOTEBOOK

OUT
BASKET

IN   OUT

BINDER

$

TRASH

BINDER
CONTAINS:
• CURRENT JOB ORDERS
• INTERVIEW SCHEDULE
• JOB ORDER LOG
• SCORE BOARD
• MASTER LIST FOR CANDIDATES
• FIRST INTERVIEW PHONE LIST
• UNITED STATES MAP

DRAWER 1
LISTS:
• CANDIDATE LISTS
• CLIENT CONTACT LIST
• DIRECTORIES
• PRAYER BOOK

DRAWER 2
FILES:
• JOB ORDER FORMS
• INVOICE FORMS
• INTERVIEW FORMS

DRAWER 3
• CURRENT RESUMES
• 4X6 CLIENT CARDS

DRAWER 4
• THANK-YOU NOTES
• ENVELOPES
• BROCHURES/BUSINESS CARDS
• DICTIONARY/THESAURUS
• PORTABLE TAPE RECORDER
• TOOTHBRUSH
• POWER BARS

155

Do you need a computer? Some say yes, others could care less. I use one mainly for word processing and I keep a client database current on my Secretary's/Researcher computer. I know recruiters who are fully automated and love it. If you have grown up with computers and they work for you,then it's the right way to go. If-on the other hand-you're spending more time inputting and staring at a screen, then throw it out the window and buy a three ring binder and some highlighter pens.

Everybody has 24 hours a day. It's up to you how you use them. I encourage you to carefully study where you spend your time and adjust the ratios, no matter how difficult it may be at first, to insure success in the recruiting industry. It is not that difficult to accomplish. It just takes some discipline and the courage of your convictions.

Chapter 15.
Phone techniques: Scripts To Use and Etiquette 101

Operator, can you help me place this call?

Command in using the telephone is one of the primary skills of the professional recruiter. The ability to *Think On Your Seat* and create an opportunity where one didn't exist is an art that can be learned and honed to a fine edge.

When I speak of command of the phone, I mean having an awareness of what you can accomplish with your voice, inflection, pace, authority, humor, politeness, candidness, and persistence. Command means the skills to elicit trust, goodwill, referrals, commitment and promises of future business. Rather than learning these skills through trial and error, this chapter is dedicated to sharing with you phone scripts which will teach you to anticipate what comes next and to be ready.

Even though we have covered a number of these techniques in many of the early chapters, I felt it was important to provide you with a concentrated dose of phone scripts and ideas to use in all facets of calling situations. And while no one could anticipate all the variations of what will happen when a person on the other end picks up the phone, we can make some assumptions to get you the information you need; the essence of what *Thinking On Your Seat* is all about.

Let's explore three main techniques as they relate to making connected conversation with who you are calling. They are:
1. Calls to a hiring authority; a potential client.
2. Calls to a candidate you're trying to locate and then recruit.
3. Proper phone etiquette.

> **The goal of any call you make is to get something of value from that call. Have a purpose in mind when you pick up the phone. Set an objective and visualize what you want to happen. Have a positive attitude when you call and keep that feeling throughout every call.**

Getting through the Gatekeeper

In the following examples I'll explain what the objective is of the call, then give you a short script of dialogue you can use, and finally, review what happens and why the words, inflection and pace of the call is so important.

1. Calling the potential hiring authority- a potential client.

In this example, I'll assume we have the manager's name and title. Dial the phone with three simple objectives in mind: To make connected conversation; to leave a message interesting enough to get a return call; to verify I have the right person. The phone rings:

Recruiter: Hello. Is Steve Anderson in his office today?
Gatekeeper: No, he's not. May I ask who's calling?
Recruiter: Yes, this is Russ Riendeau. Does Steve have voice mail and can you put me into it?
Gatekeeper: Certainly, hold on.

Simple enough right? Voice mail is great! I don't have to go through the interrogation of a secretary in charge of protecting the gate and screening out the calls which can waste the manager's time. So now that I'm in the voice mail, I can say whatever I need to say and the manager will hear it. The message I leave might sound like this:

Steve, good morning, my name is Russ Riendeau, **I understand** you are the vice president of sales for your company, and I would like to speak with you **regarding some business** here in the Midwest. I was referred to you by_____. **I'll be in my office today and tomorrow**, so you can call me at_____. **I look forward** to speaking with you. Goodbye.

If I was referred to the manager by someone within the company, I might introduce myself as a professional recruiter. However, if the referral is not a current peer in the company, then I will just say that I was referred and I'll explain who and why when I get the manager's return call.

Notice the bold text in this phone script.
"I understand" assures me that he is the right person. If not he will call me back and tell me who is the right individual to call.
"Regarding some business here in the Midwest" entices the manager to call me back because he isn't sure what I mean. It could mean anything and that's why he must call me. Once I speak with him I explain I'm a recruiter and go into my presentation. He can't get offended because I didn't lie about who I was; I just stated it was regarding business and it is!
"I'll be in my office today and tomorrow" gives Steve a time frame in which to call me back. It shows a sense of

urgency to the call and sends a message that I may not be there after tomorrow so he better call me or he may miss me. What if I have a big order to place?

"look forward" is stating that I expect his return call. I didn't say to call me when he has a moment, or call when you can, or, if he's not busy to give me a call. I mean business! Call me, it's important and it can't wait.

The power of the presentation is the difference between getting calls back promptly and having to call a manager six times to get a call back.

Getting through the gatekeeper-again

What if the manager doesn't have voice mail and the receptionist or secretary is your first obstacle? The call may go like this:

Recruiter: Hello. Steve Anderson please. Russ Riendeau calling. Thank you.

Gatekeeper: What company are you with?

Recruiter; Thomas Lyle and Company. Is Steve in his office?

Gatekeeper: What is this in regard to?

Recruiter: This is in regard to some business here in the Midwest. May I speak with Steve please?

Gatekeeper: What kind of business?

Recruiter: I was referred to Steve by someone within your marketplace, may I speak with Steve, or may I leave message?

Notice *I asked four times* to speak with Steve and still didn't get put through. I might have been put into Steve after the first two requests, however it could go on forever. I didn't say what I do for a living even when they asked me point blank

what kind of business I was in. At this point, the chances of getting to speak with Steve are slim, so maybe I'll try again when the gatekeeper is at lunch or late or early in the day. I may even call the company back and ask for a different department and have that department put me through to the person. It may bypass the gatekeeper and-bingo-I'm in! Or, I may cry "Uncle" to the gatekeeper and respond with this statement after I've have tried to get through to him.
"I am a management recruiter and am conducting a confidential search for a client of mine. I would like to speak with Steve to discuss the position and ask his help in referring me to a potential candidate, and I hope I can return the favor to him someday. Could you relay that message to him today? I appreciate it very much." The gatekeeper may not want to touch this one, so you may get put through right away.

The pace of the call is very critical. Whenever I asked the gatekeeper a question, I always follow up with a prompt "thank you", or, "is he in?" In this way I can control the direction of the call by not allowing the gatekeeper to formulate her own set of questions. I can direct the call in a way that I want and he or she may be intimidated enough to put the call through, or she will sense my authority and presence and do what I ask. Remember: the person in the gatekeeper role is in a hierarchical environment. In most cases, a person who can command a powerful or confident presence will get the benefit of being put through. This doesn't mean being arrogant or a bully, but being direct, firm, polite and confident will get you in more places than being milque-toast and unsure.

Important reminder: If you ever misrepresent yourself to a person on the phone in attempt to get to another person, you can be breaking the law. In addition to the legal aspect, Caller

I.D. is becoming a much-used service and if you lie, companies can find you in a hurry. Lastly, if the latter doesn't dissuade you, once the caller you intended to speak with finds out you lied to the gatekeeper to get to them, they'll not want to do business with you anyways, so why take the risk? Most people will answer your questions if you ask in a polite and direct manner.

Check with an attorney to understand your limits.

> I've always taken the approach that if I have to work that hard to get in touch with a particular manager, I could have a problem getting a call back or even getting through to them when I'm conducting a search. It may not be worth it. On the other hand, if a manager is accessible,but difficult to reach, then I will work with him because I know most recruiters will give up and I've got an inside track and a phone guard to keep out the competition.

Another approach if you can't get through

Send the manager a note that says: 'Your secretary is the best I've seen to date. I have tried for weeks to get through to you to discuss an exceptional opportunity with one of my clients. You may know somebody who fits this slot, or even you. Please call me confidentially to discuss this position and give my regards to your gatekeeper, she's the best. Best Regards." If this doesn't get a response forget it, and move on.

Calling with a referral from a peer in the same company

This call is a piece of cake. The script goes like this:
" Hello Steve, Russ Riendeau calling. I was referred to you by Bruce Wayne in your automotive division. I am a professional

recruiter and he mentioned there may be some areas I could assist you in recruiting. Please call me at _____. I look forward to your call."

2. Calling a manager when you haven't a clue where they are.

When you have a manager that you know is the one you're looking for, but can't find her in the numerous hiding spots of a corporation, try this approach with a receptionist.

Recruiter: Hello, I'm looking for your vice president of sales. Who would that be?

Receptionist: What division are you looking for?

Recruiter: I didn't realize there were so many. Where would you suggest I start?

Receptionist: What product or service are you calling about?

Recruiter: Your consumer products group.

Receptionist: That would be Ms. Higginbottom.

Recruiter: Thank you for your help. Can you put me through to her...oh by the way who is the vice president of your industrial division and healthcare groups?

Notice I simply asked the questions in a rapid-fire approach. I got the name I was looking for and then gained more names in a nonchalent fashion. Normally a receptionist won't give you the third degree when asking for the names in a large organization, so this approach is a lot easier.

Using an alias-cautiously

We all have told some white lies in our lives and the recruiting business is not exempt from these temptations as well. But when it comes to using an alias or false name to get information or contact a candidate, it is not a good idea. The

163

only time I use a different name is when I'm calling a company that I have recruited people from in the past, and should someone recognize my real name, it could put that recruit in a dangerous situation because others assume that person is looking for a job, when in fact he's not. This is the only time I suggest you consider this option to protect the confidentially of the person you're calling.

All the sample scripts I've suggested to you can be altered to suit the situation. You probably noticed that the premise of each script is to gain information and establish connected conversation ASAP. *Thinking On Your Seat* is the learned skill of going from a recruit call to getting a job order call or from a fact-finding call to a recruit call. Be ready for anything to happen, and have a phone presentation ready to use when you pick up and dial. **To think on your feet successfully is to be prepared first, by** *Thinking On Your Seat!*

**Eleven proven ideas that make cents on the phone.
Etiquette.**

Here's some quick tips to use when involved in connected conversation on the phone. The suggestions are simple, but very relevant and effective. Your livelihood depends on a professional and articulate presentation. Spend the time to learn this skill and never stop trying to improve.

1. Smile on the phone. Speak clearly and directly into the mouthpiece. Holding the phone against your shoulder with your chin distorts your voice and causes the quality of inflection and tone to suffer. Consider using a good headset if you are always scrunching the phone to your ear with your shoulder. It's easier on the neck muscles, too.

2. "Please" and "thank you" go a long way in our hurried world. They may forget your mistakes or other short-comings, **but they won't forget your rudeness**.

3. When finished with a conversation, let the other party hang up first. The folks at AT&T taught me that subconsciously people feel you're too busy to speak with them, or they feel less important if they hear your click first. We tend to forget facts first, feelings second.

4. If a call comes in for you and you're busy, unprepared or distracted, don't take the call. Ask to call the person back. Nothing is more frustrating than to have a conversation with a person who *is not* mentally there, or who's carrying on two conversations. Every call you take can be a major customer at some point.

5. If the connection is bad, don't fight it. Ask to call back.

6. Don't keep people on hold too long. What's too long? Forty five seconds can seem like an eternity on the phone. We are all guilty. Have your secretary check in with the person or get a number and call back.

7. Studies show that the third ring is the best one to answer on. Three rings gives the other party time to settle into their mode of communication while waiting for you to answer. More than three shows inattentiveness and lack of concern for the customer. Picking up on the first ring can appear disorganized, desperate and unprofessional. The only exception is if you're the 911 operator.

8. Avoid profanity at all costs, even if the other party is using it.

9. Try to create a distinct style and sound. Practice with a recorder and seek to improve clarity, warmth, depth, believability, pace, breathing, emotion, humor and mood. Does your voice match how you feel about your work, your life, and your belief in the customer's needs?

10. Take a phone skills seminar from a reputable company. AT&T still does them and Fred Pryor Seminars out of Mission Hills, Kansas is also excellent. Nightingale-Conant Corp. in Chicago 708-647-0300, has some great training cassette programs as well.

11. Keep on the subject. Respect people's time and attention. Have a plan and goal for the call and get off.

Come back to this chapter once in a while during the year and refresh yourself to these scripts and ideas. All of us get off course from time to time and fail to realize our technique and language has gotten sloppy and lazy. Sometimes all you need is to revamp your phone skills and you'll be out of that slump.

Chapter 16.
Exploring *New* Markets

One of the reasons I love the recruiting profession is that there are unlimited opportunities to seek out new business markets. Once the techniques and skills of the trade are understood, you can enter *any* market and successfully earn a nice living.

Every day another business is opening up and will need the services of a recruiter. So how do you find these new opportunities? It's simple, just look around. Read and listen. That's all there is to it. No fancy tactics. Spending some time at the library browsing the bestseller section for business may be a good idea, or seeing what new trade magazines or associations are being formed will also bring you up to date. But as a recruiter, you are privy to more information being discussed in a single day than most people are. Talk with candidates and managers about new markets. Ask them what they see are growing businesses.

If you're exploring new markets to get into, ask yourself why? Are you bored, frustrated, tired? Are you seeking new markets because of ethical beliefs about what your industry represents? Is your market that small that you've exhausted all new business ventures?

Some like it HOT. Uncovering new markets.

I've seen many people looking to chase a supposedly "hot market" only to realize they didn't like it after they got into it. They jumped without really exploring what and how it functions as it relates to recruiting. These same persons who chase hot markets are missing strong and regular business in their current markets. They've not exploited their contacts yet. They haven't practiced the art of networking within all divisions of a company. They stopped trying after a few placements and failed to keep adding value and knowledge to the client to improve their placement business.

Maybe it's time for a vacation to a sunny spot in the world? Take a week off to recharge your battery and look at the issue from another view. Try taking some time off to do something totally different from *Thinking On Your Seat* for a living. Build or take apart something, dig in the yard, or take a hike.

When I get in a funk at times, I spend time doing physical tasks which require little thought. It gets me away from the constant brain work and analysis of our business and allows me to relax and work out some frustrations. I run, build stuff, paint something, golf, plant a tree, go swim, see a ball game, ride my bike, anything that takes little conscious decision making. My wife Cheryl sees my need to take a break even before I feel it. I listen to her observations a lot more than she thinks!

If after careful consideration and reflection you still want to change markets, then go for it and don't look back. But spend enough time researching the industry and people working in that market. Check for compatibility of work ethic and styles. A friend of mine was considering entering the recruiting business and was trying to figure out what market to get into. One of the markets of interest would have involved a lot of night time calls because of the work schedules of that industry. He also learned that the people in that market were not the most conversational group of individuals, and he is a true conversationalist. Networking would have been difficult and he would have been frustrated out of his mind recruiting in that industry. He has since changed directions.

Is it the industry? Or is it you?

A new market for you to explore could be an old market. Hmmm..... you say. An old market- a new market? Yes indeed. Many industries have declined over the years in the necessity for their product or services. Industries like the glass container business are being pushed out by plastic, or the steel industry is overshadowed by new composite materials. Service industries are squeezed by the improvement of do-it-yourself applications for carpet cleaning, car washes, photography, and printing. All these industries are not growing at the same rate as years past, but still need people and are finding new ways to apply their technology and knowledge to other markets. The steel industry is finding more creative ways to coat, bend and style steel. The glass container industry is remarketing the color and beauty of glass and promoting its versatile and recyclable characteristics. The service industries are lowering prices and improving their service to make them more appealing. So you see, new methods for an old industry creates opportunities that the others are giving up on.

Are hot markets ready for you?

Sometimes new markets aren't ready for recruiters. They're still getting their feet wet and are not sure what they need. And

169

because the market is still small, they may be able to use their old network and bypass you. Only when the market gets beyond their view of who's who can you work effectively in that market. Be patient.

Chapter 17.
Consistency: Ratios And Formulas
That Work!

Successful recruiters understand there will be ups and downs in this business. The economy will play a *small* part in how much business there is at certain times of the decades, but I have found that being consistent is more than the luck of the economy. It has to do with understanding ratios of your own performance and realizing what formulas to use to maintain constant billings.

Being new to the business, you'll be at a slight disadvantage in not having past ratios and formulas to learn, but an experienced recruiter can learn a great deal about their work habits and patterns of searches. So if you're a seasoned recruiter, compare your efforts to the next part of this chapter, and if you're a new recruiter, pull aside a veteran and learn from his statisics. Let me give you some examples of what I'm referring to.

Ratios to live by as a headhunter

I have found over the years that my ratio of job orders to placements made is about 1:7. This means that for every job order that I become aware of in my field, I'll make a placement of at least 1 in 7. Some years it's higher, but over the past 11 years it's averaged to be this ratio. Your market may be different, but the key is to start tracking it by keeping a job order log.

Another ratio is the amount of job orders I can work on at one time. If I work on seven to eleven job orders per month, I'll make at least 2 placements per month. This follows the previous ratio pretty close, so I know the key to consistency is to keep the amount of job orders in that range. Any more job orders than that and I become ineffective.

I don't keep track of sendouts to placement ratios because every client is different as to how many candidates they elect to see, so I never saw much value in this ratio. I choose to concentrate my energy on getting as many sendouts as possible--solid sendouts that is--to increase my yearly billings.

I also know that the average placement takes about 45 days from the day I receive the assignment to getting an offer accepted. I can look ahead and know within a reasonable estimate how much business will close over the next three weeks.

If my billings are down in a month, I look at the number of sendouts. If the sendout numbers are average, I look at the number of job orders on my plate. If that number is average I check the *quality* of the job order and I can normally pinpoint the problem to working weak or low percentage job orders. So I get on the phone and find some better ones.

Many recruiters will fall into a comfort zone of some sort after recruiting for a few years. It happens to everybody in every business out there, so don't be alarmed. But if you get into a comfort zone, how do you increase your income without working harder or longer hours? **Simple: search for companies paying bigger fees.** I haven't talked about the size of fees much in this book because each market has its own compensation plans and histories, so quoting fee numbers to you will mean nothing, if it doesn't relate to your market. The easiest way to make more money is to say "no" to the small fees and find bigger ones. But most recruiters find it difficult to change their philosophy of working with managers and companies to get higher fees. We all know that a bigger fee is easier to work than a small one. So why not work a big one? The reason is simple: habit.

Years ago Lyle Stenfors, who hired me in 1985, pulled me in his office one day and told me I couldn't work with a particular client I had been making placements with for the past year. I was mad! "You're taking money out of my pocket" was my belief. But he was right in doing so. He encouraged me to prospect for better clients, with less turnover, and bigger fees. He was the boss, so I had no choice; but he was right. I had developed a false sense of security in working with this client because they always had an opening, but my reputation was becoming one of working with weak companies and that's bad. I went on to secure better fees, better companies and made more money as a result, and enjoyed the searches even more.

Creating a "Formula Fit" for increased placement percentages

Another method to increase your billings is to concentrate on working assignments which fit into your "formula fit" criteria for candidates and companies. In other words, continue to seek out companies where you can place the type of candidate who is typical to your area of specialization, regardless of how broad of a market you work. Let me explain. If you decide to work in the recruiting business placing outside sales professionals, you'll come to realize that the managers looking for candidates will typically look for the same type of person. These managers' qualifications can be broken down into a few categories such as:

> Age
> Martial status
> College education
> Appearance
> Income range
> Motivation to change
> Number of prior jobs out of school
> Personality
> Geographic location

Eventually you can identify a formula in your specialty, and by concentrating your efforts on recruiting and networking with individuals within this formula, you'll increase the number of placements you make on a yearly basis. Your job will become easier because you don't
have to re-invent the wheel every search. This one simple tactic in recruiting is the single most important lesson to growing your business rapidly. It is simply *Thinking On Your Seat;* anticipating what the client will need in their job openings and having a place to find these candidates quickly.

Client company formulas too!

The same methodology goes for finding fee-paying companies as well! You may find that over a short period of time the clients you work with most successfully will have their own personalities and expectations. In most cases they will continue to seek out individuals with a certain background (formula fit) and the company will fit into a formula as well. You can clone your clients to increase your placement chances. These companies will fit into a mold related to:

> .Size of organization
> .Direct contact with management or
> human resources
> .Lots of candidates with the formula you
> seek.

.Culture such as: management style,
humor, work ethic, and interview
methods.
.Growth industry or staple products
.Location of offices close to you for
personal visits
.Competitive compensation plans *above*
the industry average
.A willingness to work with recruiters
and develop a relationship
.Hires promptly; doesn't drag out
searches

If these companies start to fit a certain pattern, and you have
success in working with these types of companies, then place
your efforts in seeking out more of these types of companies.
Even if you're tempted by job orders in a different arena, the
impact of your income from billing is directly related to the
efficiency of how you work and where. The only choices you
have in relation to your time is who you work *for* and who you
work *with.* I encourage you to choose your clients carefully.

An excellent selling tool you possess when specializing with a
certain type of company is consistency and knowledge.
Companies with certain cultures and personalities are aware of
other companies within their marketplace with similar cultures
and they will realize you can help them if you have placed
individuals with their *type* of organization. "Like attracts like"
is a fact of life.

Chapter 18.
Marketing Higher-up the Organization

The big guys always call back. I wonder why?

The best way to gain access to bigger fees, consistent business, national accounts, management searches, and long-term relationships is to **complete** the searches you're given with the client as effectively and promptly as possible. Then you can earn their respect and gain an audience with the higher up. Sell the Thunder, They'll Buy the Rain.

The fact of the matter is, that no matter how good you are and how in-touch you are with the market; not too many companies are going to be willing to believe everything you say you can do and lock in a long-term agreement with a total stranger. Managers, whether they are CEO's, line managers, or customer service managers will want to see an example of your work before any lasting agreements are signed. No amount of statistics, surveys, psychological testing programs you provide, or employee evaluation guidelines will make up for your demonstrated ability to find a person they'd hire.

The top recruiters I've have worked with first concentrate on making a placement at the level they are accustomed to working in everyday. Once the placement is completed, they send thank you letters to the hiring managers, but also to their boss and their boss' boss. I call these higher up letters "good news letters." Letters that sell without selling. They may look like this:

Dear Executive Vice President,

My name is Russ Riendeau and I am a sales and management recruiter with_____. I recently had the opportunity to work with Steve Anderson in your _____division and we were able to identify a candidate for him in a short period of time. It has been a pleasure working with your organization. The promptness of Stephen's feedback related to the search, the friendly atmosphere of the corporate offices and the professionalism of the written material all contributed to the successful hire.

Should you have a need in other areas of your company, please call me directly so we can meet confidentially and discuss further ways I can be of service.

Best Regards,
Russ Riendeau

Upper management folks are even better networkers than managers below them because they know how fickle "Mahogany Row" can be. (Mahogany Row refers to the line of corporate desks at the corporate headquarters.) They stay in touch with recruiters and actually enjoy referring you to other places in the organization. It is a way for them to earn points with their peers by being in touch with good people. So every time you place someone in a company, send a good news letter to the upper managers; you may even want to call them at some point. The chances of developing a client with multiple placement opportunities starts with this strategy.

Note of caution: This *doesn't* mean calling up the CEO of Ameritech or some other high-ranking official. Use business common sense where you feel it would be appropriate to call the president or top management.

Remember, too, that these same higher up managers could be looking to make a job change sometime. They now have a go-to person (you) that can assist them should they want to leave. And then you'll have an even more loyal client if you place them.

Learn to work harder on yourself than you do on your job. This will ensure success throughout all aspects of your life.

Chapter 19.
Positive Mental Attitude

Throughout this book we've focused on the approach of being prepared, being flexible to a given situation--*Thinking On Your Seat*. However nothing positive will last without a positive attitude about what you can do and what you do for a living. If there is any common characteristic that I see among successful people; whether it be manager, sales professional, mother, father, teacher, coach, or physician, it's the optimistic belief and positive energy that they exude that creates and sustains success in their lives.

The Top 5% Club Membership: You can become a member.

What do Michael Jordan, John Grisham, Mark Twain, The President of the United States, and you all have in common? Well, if you are one of the top performers in your field of work, then you are all part of the Top 5% Club! Even though you can't write like Mark Twain, or play like Michael Jordan, they can't do what you do either! They don't have a clue how to effectively conduct a search for a vice president of marketing for a major corporation. They don't know how to recruit, evaluate, present and negotiate a compensation plan for a candidate. But you do and you can do it with the same level of expertise that these famous folks do their job effectively. The fact that they are in the public eye gives them a certain level of WOW in our minds, but remember, they have specialized knowledge just like you. They are no different in their abilities, just more publicized in their field.

> You deserve to have success in your life. No one can
> take away the effort and energy you put into what you
> do. And if that success comes to you in the form of
> compensation, status, freedom of expression and time
> off to relax, then enjoy it because you've earned it.
> Have faith in the free enterprise system of this country.
> If you provide a product or service that satisfies a need for a
> lot of people, you're entitled to be compensated for
> it handsomely.

The $1,000,000 paint brush

Having confidence in your ability and clearly defined goals
will have a greater impact on your future than you realize. I
realized this fact years ago, when I was working full time for
a home developer in the Chicago suburbs. I was newly married
and was doing side jobs painting houses to earn some extra
cash, plus I was getting bored with my daytime job and needed
a diversion. I ended up painting the home of an executive with
Federal Express. He took a liking to me and asked what I was
doing painting houses. When I told him my plans to get into
sales and leave the building industry, he suggested I come and
interview with Fed Ex. So I did.

The interview went well, however the possibility of numerous
relocations with the company over a career was a must and I
was not interested in relocating, so I passed on the possibility
of joining the company, When leaving the Fed Ex office after
one of these interviews,, I came down the elevator and saw a
sign that read "Thomas Lyle & Company" in the window of an
office in the same building. I stopped in and asked what they
did and was given Lyle Stenfors card. We met a few weeks

later and became fast friends. Two years later, I went to work for Lyle and Tom Beamer (a partner as well) at Thomas Lyle & Company, as a sales recruiter. And over the next seven years, I billed over a million dollars in fees. The million dollar paint brush.

This story demonstrated to me the power of conviction and purpose. There was something that the Fed Ex manager saw in me that gave him the courage to refer me to his company. I could have made him look like a turkey if I wasn't close to what the company needed. Yet he had confidence that I was the right caliber. Had he not given me that chance, I would have never met Lyle, wouldn't be aware of the recruiting industry, and you would not be reading this book. If all these pieces of the puzzle had not been put into place by some divine order, my life would be very different. *The power of purpose is an awesome principle.*

The power of conviction and the purpose of your role as a successful recruiter must be transmitted to the client. And this can be transmitted through your enthusiam and follow-up, promptness and feedback, effective communication and professional-looking written materials, and personal visits. People can feel and sense a passion, a conviction or deeply seated belief in another person. Do you have that passion for your business today? Do you really get charged-up and have that sense of urgency to make things happen today? If you do, then managers and candidates you work with will want to be on your ship when the waters are rough. And this same conviction will carry you through lean times in business climates that sour. The same energy you exhibit today will attract your future candidates and clients for tomorrow. Enjoy yourself today.

Chapter 20:
Personal Development and On-Going Training

What you learn is related to how much you earn.

The recruiting profession, like any other career, demands a certain amount of on-going training and personal development to stay current and fresh. Your family physician, dentist, landscaper and fireman all have to keep up with technological advances in their craft or else they can't do their job properly.

And so it is with recruiting. Maintaining your edge as a successful recruiter has its own set of disciplines. Over the years I have met numerous successful recruiters from all over the country and the one thing that stands out in my observations of these individuals is that they are always doing and trying new things in life. Whether it's sports-related, reading new information, exploring, hiking, the arts, collecting, volunteering--they are continually seeking out a means of expression and discovery. Maybe this is the natural curiosity of people who enter the recruiting profession; a deep down urge to find the answer regardless of what it is they are searching for. I know that as a kid I always wanted to be an FBI agent. This business of recruiting allows me to be a part-time investigator, only I look for the *good guys*.

To maintain a positive, fresh, and current view of the business world, family life, and just a general sense of well-being, I've compiled a list of topic areas to be aware of in your personal development quest throughout a lifetime of being a professional recruiter. These subjects are diverse and some are very different from what you may have considered important in the past, however with the world becoming a tighter community of diverse lifestyles, it's important to look at things with a very different and open mind. Here's the list, certainly not a complete list, but one that should keep you busy for a while. Try to find time to read, listen, attend seminars and take classes on subjects such as:

Behavioral psychology
Memory training
Rapid reading techniques
Growing your vocabulary
Communication skills in letter writing
The aging of Americans--Demographics
Sales training and Effective negotiating
Listening skills/Interpersonal communication
Cultural diversity
Wealth management
Personal health management/Hobbies
Recruiter and consultant training

If you can devote just *thirty* minutes a day to these subject areas, you'll continue to see improvement, not only in your recruiting abilities, but in your overall attitude. You'll begin to have more confidence, more time to do what you want, you'll be more relaxed, you'll be sought out for your insights into helping to solve problems, and you'll feel up-to-date with what's happening in the world today. **Reading this book is already a great step forward!**

Physical fitness is another critical area of your personal development quest. Exercise builds stamina and endurance of mind and body. Exercise rids the body of toxins and excess weight you don't need. Regular exercise has also been proven to; reduce stress, improve your attention span, sex life, outlook on life in general, and reduce the numerous ailments that are just plain annoying. I encourage you to find a way to budget in exercise three times a week for at least twenty minutes. The benefits will astound you.

When we realize that we know very little about our world, we then become a student of life, rather than expecting the world to conform to our wishes.

How much is enough learning?

I don't know what it is for most, but I try to read at least 12-16 books per year, either on tape or word by word. I read at least eight monthly publications per month in the form of business magazines, newsletters, trade journals, Wall Street Journal, business papers, and magazines related to my primary hobbies and sports preferences such as aviation, motorcycles, running, writing, and woodworking. I try to throw in some classic literature to expand my vocabulary and stretch my imagination as well. Your list may be more or less than mine, but we all have priorities in learning. The important thing is to do something to keep yourself growing and learning; to expand your frame of reference outside the little box you live in.

Realize that what you do and say
really does have an impact
on other peoples' lives.

Chapter 21.
Working With Other Recruiters-- Networking For Profit

Working with other recruiters around the country is another way to increase your yearly billings and improve your placement percentages.

Throughout the country there are numerous organized networks of participating recruiting companies who join forces to create a tight group specializing in one or many different markets. It could be sales, technical support, engineering, marketing, insurance, physicians, nurses, landscapers, you name it. These networks operate on a split-fee basis, enabling you to make placements for your client company in parts of the country where you're not able to effectively find a candidate quickly. And even though you are splitting the fee with the recruiter you contacted, it's worth it to you because you may have never filled the position anyway; the recruiter on the receiving side of your call may have never heard of the opening and is glad to get your call; and the client is happy as can be because they have one person, you, whom they can call to fill openings for their company anywhere in the country. National account contracts here we come!

The recruiting firm you currently work for may already be part of some affiliate network, like the one our company has been involved in for the past 18 years, The First Interview

Network, created by my good friend Bob Mikesell in Atlanta, Georgia. His number by the way is 770-952-1058, should you want to explore your options of this network primarily for sales recruitment. The National Association of Personnel Services 703-684-0180, can also help to find a network that suits your needs.

Trick of the trade:

One way to find more recruiters that specialize in your market is to contact major corporations in various parts of the country and speak with the human resource department. Ask them who they have worked with in the past to recruit the type of persons you recruit. They will typically have a few recruiters in their files and be happy to give you names and numbers. Then contact that recruiting firm and find the person who works that market to see if you are compatible in work style, energy level, ethics, and professionalism. You may want to ask for a few references of other recruiters they have worked with in the past to get a better read. And these references could be additional recruiters for you to network with! See how the system works so beautifully?

The one potential downfall of working with another recruiter is that the fee is split. You and they are working for half of what you typically earn and that can be financially hard to swallow. So how do you create a level of commitment from that recruiter to give his or her best effort, and best candidates, to your search assignment? And how do you convince your *client* that your affiliate will work as hard for half the fee, and provide the best candidates? This can be a very sensitive subject with a manager who has heard this story before.

If you have worked with the recruiter affiliate before, you have probably set up a good working relationship with them by now. To instill confidence in your client's minds, educate them on how your network functions. Talk about past successes and mention other clients who have taken advantage of your ability to help them all over the United States. Consider having them speak personally with your affiliate to feel comfortable that they are as competent as you. This also gets the client involved more deeper into the partnership.

Here's a few secrets to improve the chances of your affiliate filling the position you send:
1. Send the affilate a solid search assignment, not a hope and a prayer opening. A good recruiter can smell a waste of time for miles. Make sure the specs are realistic, (remember the 12 point checklist in Chapter 6) the fee is large enough to allow the recruiter to make it worth the effort, offer access to the hiring manager, if possible, to improve communication and allow the affilate to expand the specs to better understand the assignment. Try to have some firm interview dates already scheduled with the manager before you call the affiliate with the opening.

2. Keep the affiliate posted on what is happening if they are only supplying you candidates that you then contact and present to your client. Inform them of changes in the client's requirements, interview style and sense of urgency, to get the recruiter to pinpoint exactly the profile needed.

3. If the search is dropped, fades away, or becomes unrealistic to fill, call that recruiter and cancel the search. The best way to have a recruiter never work hard for you again is to not tell him when a search is history. No one likes to work for free.

4. When you receive a search assignment from an affiliate recruiter, be upfront and tell the recruiter if you can and will aggressively work the opening. If the search is out of your expertise, or the fee is ridiculiously low, or you are swamped with too many searches already, tell him so and encourage him to still call you in the future. He will call you again if you approach it in this manner. However, if you take the assignment and don't work it, he'll never call you again.

Networking with other recruiters is a great way to improve the service you provide for your clients and a way to generate additional income for you and your firm. You'll also make some great friendships with persons all over the country, and world, once you start to network internationally.

Chapter 22.
Tools and Forms For Staying Organized

Keeping track of your activity, both current and past, is critical to your effectiveness as a recruiter and to your professionalism with the client and candidate. We are all skeptical of working with people who appear to be unsure of what's happening, especially when they're in charge!

These forms should give you some help in keeping track of your activity related to interviews, job orders you have farmed out, client information, and job order logs to follow-up for additional business. You have my permission to copy these forms out of this book and use for them your own use. **The key to their effectiveness is to actually use them every day.**

  Form 1. Weekly activity sheet. Use this to keep track of who is interviewing with what company, status of the interview process and comments for future use. You can also keep information such as, interview locations and key phone numbers related to the search including hotel numbers where the client is staying, street addresses, and additional persons the candidate will meet at the interview. I personally save these forms for a year to use as references to possible candidates for *future* assignments and to check my placement vs. sendout ratios.

Form 2. Job order log. Every job assignment you come in contact with gets noted on this log. The date, company, position, fee quoted, what affiliate you split it out to if applicable, and general comments. This log is critical to seeing trends in your searches, keeping track of client companies for future business, and is a way to check with the client six months down the road to see if the assignment is still open, or if maybe they re-contacted one of your candidates and hired them. It's happened to many recruiters and they never would have learned of the placement if they'd not kept a job order log to refer back to. I am lost without it.

Form 3. Brainstorm sheet. A piece of paper with nine equal boxes on it to act as a holding place for you to write down names of potential candidates for assignments. This acts as an idea sheet to see what candidates could fit into other job openings you're working on. You may see a candidate fitting into another job when you see the names and openings all together. It's also a good tool to keep for future reference, to see what types of candidates a client looked at in the past, and for ideas to find additional candidates.

Form 4. Client contact card. If you don't use a computer to keep track of your clients, this method is probably the most used organization tool in the business. Simply create a 4x6 note card with all the pertinent information about your client that you need. The front side has all the basics including name, address, and numbers to reach them. The back holds the critical information relating to the manager's background, hiring style, organization chart, number and location of personnel they manage, competitors, sources to find candidates and an ideal profile they would hire in a minute. If you keep this card up-to-date you will place people with that manager guaranteed, as long as they work with recruiters. (And remember, we said if they *don't* use recruiters, they *don't* get into your client file.)

These are the key forms I encourage you to use in your daily activity. Keep them in a three ring binder or manila file which is cleaned out weekly and stocked with fresh forms. It takes discipline to get into the habit of using this system, or any system for that matter, so be patient and consistent. It will pay big dividends.

Here are the forms for your use on the following pages.

Weekly Activity Sheet

Interview date/time   Candidate   Client company   Comments

196

Job Order Log Book

Date   Company   Job Title $ Fee Split in/out -who

Brainstorm Sheet
Use full sheet of paper divided into 12 equal boxes

Company   Company   etc.
Possible candidates   Possible candidates

_____

4X6 Client Contact Card
**Create a card for every company you call that _uses_
recruiters.**

Front of card   **Back of card**
-Corporation   **Information on**
                                           - sales reps. and location
-Division   -Manager background
-Manager Name & Title   -Personal insight:
                                   -family, hobbies, neighborhood etc.
-Address   -Preferences, pet
                                           peeves
-Phone/Fax/ Voice mail   -Ideal profile of candidate
                                     they'd hire or interview
-Secretary's Name if applicable   -Other referrals to
                                           divisions
                                     -Competitors and source
                                     companies or industries
                                           - Any info you
                        feel important enough *not* to forget

Never trust your memory. Whenever you get a idea, write it down wherever you're at and act on it ASAP!

*Chapter 23.
Special Section: For Owner/Managers On Selecting And Hiring Recruiters for *Your* Company.

Recruiting is easy; hiring recruiters is tough.

The toughest assignment for any owner or manager of a recruiting firm or placement agency is the duty of selecting and hiring recruiters. This business is filled with the widest array of personalities, styles, work habits, and personal philosophies I've ever seen. So how do you identify and make decisions of who comes to work for you? Your guess is as good as mine, however here are some ideas to keep in mind as you're interviewing and sizing up a person's qualifications. These ideas are intended to stimulate you to consider all options of personalities, knowing yourself that the majority of us come from a wide berth of backgrounds. Anybody with any background can do this business if they are committed and more importantly , have a burning desire to constantly make things happen where there was nothing before.

15 ideas to increase your odds of making a good decision

1. Look for demonstrated independence. Are they a free thinker, or do they look for the final, final, final word on things before making a decision?

2. Self-reliance. Have they "found their own way" in the past?

3. Look for a little craziness. Not a full blown nut case, but a person who looks at the world with a healthy perspective and understands life is unpredictable. Can they see the value of humor in a given situation, and find a lesson in a unhappy event? Discuss their experiences in school and social parameters to see the character and direction of their peers. This information can give you insight to where their reference points come from.

4. Thick-skinned. Can they take "no" for an answer and keep going? The ninty-pound weakling with an attitude goes a long way in this business.

5. An alert mind. Can they think on their feet and can they grasp the concept of *Thinking On Your Seat?*

6. A strong, positive phone voice. Conduct an extensive interview with them on the phone. If they can present a positive, energetic profile on the phone, then a weaker face-to-face interview may not be a true indicator of their ability to be a recruiter.

7. Proven work ethic.

8. Earned their stripes. Have they worked hard in the past to get what they have? There are no handouts in recruiting.

9. Hungry. Does money turn them on? Do they need to make the sale, close the deal, get the signature today to feel good about themselves? Are they competitive? Then they will like recruiting.

10. Give them a personality profile assessment. Psychological profiles are subject to a lot of interpretation, and in most cases the person reading the assessment isn't qualified enough to really understand what it is they're reviewing. Read the results carefully being aware that you not read what you want to read into the report. Use the assessment as a guide, as a second opinion. The test shouldn't make the decision for you one way or another. Compare the results with your intuition, reference checks, and insight from the others interviewing them.

11. Let them convince you. As a recruiter, you could get anybody excited about this business and what it can be. However painting an exciting and pretty picture to a candidate could mask if they truly want to get into recruiting. Let them tell you what they see as potential in recruiting. Why does it intrigue them and what would they do to become a success? If they really check out the industry they'll find most of the pitfalls; then see if they still are jumping up and down to start.

12. Don't follow a formula. Experiment with experience levels, backgrounds, personalities, and lifestyles. Just when you think your formula is perfect, someone comes along that defies the formula and is even better than the formula that worked in the past. Be open-minded.

13. Spend time with them. Conduct at least three, maybe four, interviews at different times and even different places. See how they are in social situations, one-on-one, and see how adaptable they are. Do they have social awareness, manners, and maturity.

14. If you think they'd be tough to manage, they're probably a better risk than the conformist and the good direction follower.

15. Always check references. And don't stop until you hear something negative about them. No one is that perfect!

Hiring the physically challenged

I've been surprised as to how few recruiters there are that are disabled in some way. Our industry provides a tremendous forum for those who have physical limitations. With needing only the physical ability of a clear speaking voice, alert mind, the ability to read, and good communication skills, a person can start in the recruiting profession immediately. You can even work out of the home.

As a hiring manager, you may want to investigate within your community, a source of candidates who have the abilities we've talked about. These individuals are always seeking a way to contribute and earn a great income, as many people who are disabled were full-time working people who now can't go back to their former jobs. Consider starting this person out as a reasearcher to see if they like the job, then move then into full-time recruiting.

When I was a kid I was the one always organizing the neighborhood baseball and football games in the park. Seeing as I was the organizer, I was always picked to be a captain of one of the teams and had to pick my team from the line of kids playing. I liked the leadership role as a kid, but never liked picking players. I was uncomfortable with making those with less athletic skills stand in line knowing they would be picked last. I remember that feeling really bothering me.

So what I started to do was to pick the lesser-talented players first. This saved me from the bad feelings I'd felt before; it motivated the players I picked because they had new-found confidence and a team that actually wanted them; and it took the pressure off of us having to win, because nobody thought we had a chance with the group of weaker players. Well, the results were surprising. We WON a majority of the games! Our teams played with such passion, such enthusiasm and teamwork, that we performed better as a team than the team with the superstars and the show-offs. **They expected to win, but we wanted to win.**

This experience of team building gave me an appreciation later in life of not just looking at the outside appearance of people. Look into the heart and soul; see what is really important to them and their need to express themselves and be part of a bigger picture. Give them a chance to excel .

Be a kid again and remember the faces of your friends on that playground and recall who went on to attain success in their lives. In many cases it was the person who didn't have the presence and confidence as a child, but had the brains, heart and ability to think.

Best of luck to you in all life's events.

**Enthusiasm is the
equalizer to gifted talent.**

A PERSONAL NOTE TO THOSE CAREER SEEKERS DISABLED AND PHYSICALLY CHALLENGED.

The world of professional recruiting could be a dynamic career option for those of you who are disabled or physically challenged. And while some of you may be unable to operate in this type of environment due to physical limitations, or that you just don't care to, it may be worth investigating.

Professional recruiting is probably one of the most adaptable businesses to start in because the major components of the career revolve around a phone and a desk. Research can be done on the phone, the internet, and the United States mail. And an even greater benefit is the income potential is lucrative enough for you to invest in some specialized training in recruitment and human resource management. (It's not unusual for a first year recruiter earning over $45,000.)

If you have command of your voice, can speak clearly, have the ability to make and take phone calls, and have a general understanding of our business world, you can succeed in the recruiting profession--*if you dedicate yourself to learning the skills necessary to become a professional.* This book is a perfect start for you.

I would encourage you to explore the world of recruiting with an open mind and see if some of the local recruiting companies and employment agencies in your area are in need of researchers, recruiters, or trainees. If you find no one having openings, consider starting your own business and work out of your home. You may even qualify for some financial assistance from the Federal Government for you to start your own business if you are disabled. The Human Resource industry may be a possible career for you as well.

In 1982, I had just run my first 26-mile marathon in Chicago. A few months after that event I began having difficulty breathing when I was running. I wrote the discomfort off to a cold or allergies, but the condition persisted and I was forced to see a doctor. After getting several opinions, I was told I had asthma. Me? Asthma? Can't be. I've never had a problem with breathing, and now at age 24 I develop this? This really stinks, I thought. It's not fair.

Well, for the next seven years I could run no more than a mile or two at a time without becoming nauseated and sick. I needed constant medication to feel comfortable and my ability to engage in any kind of sporting event beyond table tennis was limited. And my mental attitude was not as positive as it should have been as well. Fortunately for me, self-educating myself about asthma and how to live with it did improve my condition I slowly became better. And to make a long story short, as of this writing I am able to run nearly unlimited miles, with little or no medication required.

I share this story with you not to undermine your particular illness or disability. Chances are your case is more severe than mine was, otherwise you may not be considering this book and a new career. I share this story with you because I learned during my stint with this serious illness-or disability-I had to do a lot of things for myself that I felt others should help me with. But that didn't happen. I finally realized that I had to take responsibility for what happens in my life; to be proactive in creating positive events to become a reality. Maybe you have felt this way too. I can understand how you feel.

> This profession, this book may be a new lease on life for you. It could help you regain some of your independence, restore your self-confidence, remove the doubt in your mind that you can contribute to your life's long term plan. *And to earn a living far better than you may have been able to make in your previous job. Man, wouldn't that be nice?* (It's not unusual for a first year recruiter to earn over $45,000.)

I wish you the best, and please write me to let me know of your successes, so I can share them with others like yourself.

RECOMMENDED READING

Power of Positive Thinking, Norman Vincent Peale, 1992 Fawcett

Think and Grow Rich, Napoleon Hill, 1987 Fawcett

Laws of Success, Napoleon Hill, 1969 Success Unlimited Inc.

Understanding Culture's Influence on Behavior, Richard Brislin, 1993 Harcourt Brace & Company

The 7 Habits of Highly Effective People, Stephen Covey, 1990 Simon & Schuster Trade

The Psychology of Winning, Denis Waitley, 1984 Berkley

Leaders, Warren Bennis and Burt Nanus, 1985 Harper & Row

What Color is Your Parachute?: A Practical Manual For Job-Hunters & Career Changers, Richard B. Boles, 1993 Ten Speed Press

The Placement Strategy Handbook, Paul A. Hawkinson and Jeffrey G. Allen, 1990 Search Research Institute

Spin Selling, Neil Rackham, 1988 McGraw-Hill

7 Kinds of Smart, Thomas Armstrong, 1993 Penguin

Thriving On Chaos, Tom Peters, 1987 Knopf

The One-Minute Manager, Kenneth Blanchard and Spencer Johnson, 1987 Berkley

See You At The Top, Zig Ziglar, 1975 Pelican

The Fordyce Letter, Paul Hawkinson 314-965-3883

Reniassance in Recruiting: 58 Strategies To Attract & Retain Elite Sales Professionals, 1996 Thomas Lyle & Company (Booklet)

Sharkproof, Harvey Mackay, 1993 HarperCollins

Consultants News, Kennedy Publications 800-531-0007

You'll See It When You Believe It, Dr. Wayne Dyer, 1989 Avon Books

Sein Language, Jerry Seinfeld, 1993 Bantam Books

Lead The Field, Earl Nightingale, Nightingale-Conant Corporation, Niles, IL. Audio Program

How To Master Your Time, Brian Tracy, Nightingale-Conant Corporation, Niles, IL. Audio Program

APPENDIX A

United States Map--Keep it in front of you as a reminder to explore other parts of the country you can help your clients fill openings.

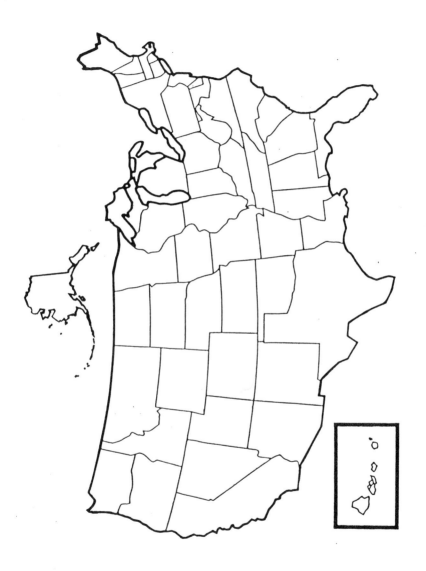

APPENDIX B
Sample letter of acceptance.

If your candidate is unsure how to word a letter of this nature, use this as a guide.

Dear New Employer,

It is with great excitement that I accept your offer of employment. The opportunity you've provided me with the ABC Company should be a great challenge and affords a great deal of growth potential.

As agreed, my starting salary will be $50,000, and a bonus potential of 30%. A company car will be provided, and the insurance program, vacation policy, and 401K information I have received in the mail.

I look forward to becoming a part of the team and will report to work on_____.

Best Regards,

APPENDIX C
Sample letter of resignation.

Most candidates are uncomfortable writing a resignation letter. They'd rather speak directly to the boss. That's fine, however make sure a official letter lands in the candidate's personnel file for future record. Suggest that the candidate deliver this letter at the time of resignation and mail a copy to human resource, to put directly into the file.

Dear Former-Employer,

I am sorry to inform you of my resignation from The ABC Company. My last day will be June 1st of this year.

The decision to leave was a difficult one, however I feel the need to expand my business experience outside this organization, develop new skills and experience diverse corporate cultures.

I will miss the people I work with, and hope to retain these friendships for a long time. To allow a smooth transition, I'll be happy to spend the time to brief my replacement.

Continued success to you and the ABC Company, and should any questions arise after I am gone, I'd be happy to answer them.

Sincerely,

cc: current supervisor
    human resource manager
    personal file at home

APPENDIX D

TELEPHONE REFERENCE CHECK

Name of
Applicant_____Date_____
Person contacted_____Title/Relationship to
applicant_____

1. Employment dates given

2. What was the nature of their work?

3. Results compared to others?

Discuss their:

4. Initiative/enthusiasm

5. Communication skills

6. Written skills

7. Were they on-time for work?

8. Strongest points in their personality

9. Strongest points in their work habits

10. Weak areas to improve on

continued

11. Any unique stories to show a special or different side of the candidate relating to his/her interaction with customers and peers?

12. If you were their new boss, How would you bring out the best in their abilities?

13. Is there anything additional you feel is important for their new employer to be aware of?

Note: add more questions which relate to skills and traits needed in your marketplace.

Since 1975, Thomas Lyle & Company has been in the professional recruiting business, specializing in recruitment of sales and management professionals on a contingent and retainer basis. Markets covered include: healthcare, medical, consumer, telecommunications, packaging, plastics, and financial markets.

About the author

Russ Riendeau is a partner and full-time recruiter with Thomas Lyle & Company, based in Palatine Illinois, a sales and management recruiting firm conducting contingency and retainer searches. Since entering the industry in 1985, Russ has consistently ranked in the top 4% of America's contingency recruiters, and being awarded six Golden Circle Awards and three Top Industrial Recruiter Awards by the First Interview Network. He has also appeared in *The Wall Street Journal, Sales & Marketing Magazine,* Nightingale-Conant audio magazine, *INSIGHT*, and *The Fordyce Letter.* A respected seminar leader to the recruiting industry, he also consults with client companies on business issues relating to compensation program design for sales organizations and recruitment profile strategies. Russ holds a Bachelor's degree in applied behavioral sciences from National-Louis University in Evanston, IL. He lives in Barrington Illinois, with his wife Cheryl and their two children.

*If you are interested in a Thinking On Your Seat
specialized workshop for your firm, please can contact him
at 847-991-5050, fax 847-991-5095, or write to:*
Russ Riendeau
Thomas Lyle & Company
16 South Bothwell
Palatine, IL 60067

-Idea page-

more ideas

_____
_____
_____
_____
_____
_____
_____
_____
_____
_____
_____
_____
_____
_____
_____
_____
_____
_____
_____
_____
_____
_____
_____
_____
_____
_____
_____
_____